WORKING
AT HUMAN
RELATIONS

2nd Edition

Rosemary T. Fruehling
Neild B. Oldham

PARADIGM

Project Editor   **Jeffrey W. Josephson**
Editorial Services   **The Oldham Publishing Service**
Cover Design   **Heidi Libera**
Composition   **The Oldham Publishing Service**
Illustrator   **Jackie Urbanovic**

Library of Congress Cataloging-in-Publication Data

Fruehling, Rosemary T.
    Working at human relations / Rosemary T. Fruehling and Neild B. Oldham.
       p. cm.
    Summary: A guide to effective interaction with others in a work situation, as well
    as in daily life.
    ISBN 1-56118-070-X
    1. Vocational guidance.   2. Interpersonal relations.
    3. Psychology, Industrial.   [1. Interpersonal relations.
    2. Vocational guidance.]   I. Oldham, Neild B. II. Title.
    HF5381.2.F76   1990
    650.1'3--dc20   90-14265
                                                   CIP
                                                      AC

10 9 8 7 6 5 4 3

TABLE OF CONTENTS

ABOUT THE AUTHORS

Dr. Rosemary T. Fruehling is an internationally known educator and lecturer in the field of business education and has taught office education at both the high school and the postsecondary levels. She has also conducted business education teacher-training seminars for the U.S. Department of Defense and for the McGraw-Hill International Division.

Dr. Fruehling has served as a consultant to such business firms as Honeywell, General Mills, International Milling, Crocker Banks, and Warner-Lambert Pharmaceutical Company. In addition, Dr. Fruehling served as Director of the Office of Software Technology Development for the State of Minnesota. Before that appointment, she was Postsecondary Vocational Education Section Manager, in the Division of Vocational-Technical Education of the Minnesota State Department of Education.

Dr. Fruehling is coauthor of other publications with Paradigm Publishing International, among them, *Your Attitude Counts, Psychology: Human Relations and Work Adjustment*, Seventh Edition, *Business Correspondence: Essentials of Communications*, Fourth Edition, *Business Communication: A Problem-Solving Approach*, Fourth Edition, and *Electronic Office Procedures*.

Dr. Fruehling received her B.S., M.A., and Ph.D. degrees from the University of Minnesota in Minneapolis.

Neild B. Oldham is a professional writer and consultant specializing in education. He has taught computers and writing at the Mitchell Junior College in Connecticut. He has also taught book publishing at the college level and currently owns and operates the Oldham Publishing Service. Before that, he was Director of Editorial Services, School Division, McGraw-Hill Book Company.

In collaboration with other educators he has written several high school and college-level textbooks. Mr. Oldham is coauthor of *Your Attitude Counts* and *Psychology: Human Relations and Work Adjustment*, Seventh Edition. He is also co-author of two English as a Second Language textbooks.

Mr. Oldham received a B.S. in Journalism from Boston University.

PREFACE

Work? Who needs it? The answer is just about all of us, if not for the work itself, then for what we get from it: a sense of identity, prestige, a feeling of doing something, and, of course, money. Most people work for money to buy the things they need—food, shelter, and clothing; and the things they want—a new car, a vacation, and better food, shelter, and clothing.

Many factors contribute to being successful at work: having the necessary technical skills, education, and experience, and, what is also important, knowing how to relate well to other people. As you will learn in this book, human relations affect all aspects of work.

Once people had little choice in the kind of work they did. Many were prevented from getting better jobs because they could not get the necessary training or education, because they were discriminated against, because they had disabilities. Many people went into the same line of work that others in their family did. Today people have greater freedom to select the job they want.

Today people want and expect different things from work, such as personal satisfaction and a means of expressing themselves. Although even the most interesting jobs have boring moments, if you plan early and well, you can find jobs that will allow you to learn, grow, and build a satisfying career.

People also work because work broadens their sense of identity. "I'm not just Jane, I'm Jane the carpenter" or "I'm John the mechanic." People identify with their careers, and their careers give them a sense of belonging or importance. To a certain extent, what people do at work determines their spare time activities, their friends, and where they live.

The terms *work*, *job*, and *career* refer to what you do to earn a living. *Work* can take place in school, office or factory, at home, or outdoors. It can be done for money, for experience, or on a volunteer basis. *Job* generally refers to an activity performed for pay.

Career, while relating to a job for pay, means more. It is the pattern of work you choose during a lifetime and it reflects your personality, interests, and lifestyle. Career suggests looking ahead, planning, and setting goals. A well-planned career is an important part of your life.

You do work, you take a job, but you *choose* and *plan* a career. The process begins in school where you learn about different career choices. You learn about yourself, your interests, your abilities, your needs, your values, and your goals.

Human relations enters into this process of building a career. You will learn that human relations has to do with developing a sense of self-awareness and of the forces that shape you; it has to do with communicating; it has to do with motivation, morale, and stress; and it has to do with working and getting along in a society that is a rich mixture of people from many different backgrounds and cultures, with many different personalities, talents, and interests.

UNIT 1

HUMAN RELATIONS AND YOU

After completing this unit, you will be able to:

➤ *Define human relations.*

➤ *Recognize how human relations affects your career.*

➤ *Use knowledge about yourself in human relations.*

➤ *Use your understanding of others in human relations.*

The concept of *human relations* may seem remote to you—something about which corporations worry, or that politicians talk about, or with which upcoming video stars concern themselves. Perhaps you think it is something for teachers to talk about in the classroom. Whatever it is, you might believe, it does not have much to do with you—your everyday life. If you do indeed think this—you are mistaken.

Even if you do not think entirely this way and you do have an idea that understanding concepts of human relations can have a bearing on your life, you still might not realize the full extent to which grasping human relations concepts can influence your education, job, career, and satisfaction.

Understanding concepts of human relations is important because human relations are part of your everyday life.

Think about it. What does human relations really involve? Do you realize that you are involved in human relations right now? As you read this page, you are taking part in one form of human relations—*communication.* You are receiving a message that the writer has delivered. True, the action of the writer took place some time ago, whereas your action is taking place now. Still, writer and reader are involved in human relations.

This illustrates a point about human relations to keep in mind: An act that has taken place at an earlier time can affect human relations in the present.

Take another example. On your way to school or work today, you most likely were involved in human relations. Saying hello to your friend or your teacher or the bus driver is a form of communication and thus human relations.

All forms of communication involve human relations. Whether you write, read, speak, or use sign language, you are involved in human relations. These are all forms of what might be called *direct communication.*

Direct communication is not the whole story of human relations. You constantly communicate with people indirectly in many ways. You communicate indirectly—relate to others—in how you dress, in how you take care of your body, in how you view your work and yourself. This *indirect communication* affects the quality of your human relations as much as direct communication. Both kinds are influenced by your feelings about others and about yourself.

When relating indirectly, however, you may not be as aware of the impression you are conveying. You may have human relations problems if you are unaware of what you are communicating—directly or indirectly—or how you are relating to other people. This does not mean that you should become self-conscious in your dealings with other people. You want to be comfortable and natural so people believe you enjoy spending time with them.

But you should be aware of the effect you have on others. People who bore others by talking too much or by talking only about themselves are obviously unaware of the impression they are making.

Good human relations requires that you care about others and that you have enough self-awareness to judge your effect on other people. In this crowded, complex world, you are relating to other people all the time. It is only common sense to develop good human relations that will produce the effects you want.

Many people feel that effective human relations depends on common sense. There is truth in that, but it does not follow that you can always just rely on your instincts or "gut reaction."

A great deal of what is called common sense can be learned, developed, and sharpened. Your goal in this unit is to develop and sharpen your common-sense approach to human relations.

Chapter 1

RELATING TO OTHERS

After completing this chapter, you will be able to:

➤ *Recognize the importance of good human relations skills to success in your chosen career.*

➤ *Identify the role of human relations in different careers.*

Getting along with people may not be the only important thing in life. But whatever life is all about, you will enjoy it more if you do get along with people. That is because human beings are social animals.

In today's world, you have to depend on other people from birth on. How others react to you and how you react to them will affect how you will succeed in every area of your life.

This dependence on others is particularly strong in the pursuit of a career. Few occupations can be followed in isolation. Even solitary careers—such as writing or painting—require the individual to make contacts with others. In most careers, of course, contact with others is an everyday occurrence.

We would all like to think that success can be achieved by skill or hard work alone. We do not want to believe that someone can get ahead simply by being well liked or lucky. Actually, many factors play a part in a person's success.

Someone who works hard and has talent probably will be a success to some degree, whether or not he or she has good human relations. And someone with little or no skills and lazy habits may enjoy considerable success just by being charming and by having good human relations.

However, successful people in either category are rare. Most people fall somewhere between these two extremes. That is, they do not have enough talent to ensure success in spite of getting along poorly with other people. Nor are they charmers who can succeed in a career without real technical skills and human relations skills.

Being True To Yourself

You probably have heard the old saying "To get along, you must go along." This suggests that to succeed you must do what the majority wants or what the boss wants, no matter what your own feelings and moral code demand. This is not true. It presents a false picture of human relations.

You will hear many such sayings in life. Ignore them. They block good human relations by making you think in worn-out, simple-minded ways. Each situation and each person is a little different.

Draw upon your past experiences to deal with each new situation and person, but always be alert for differences. Compare new situations and persons with those you have known in the past. Use that experience to guide your actions now, but be sure you look to see what is different in the new situation. Then you can respond and handle the new situation.

Old sayings aside, it is possible to disagree without being disagreeable. You can succeed without going along, without denying your *values* (the standards by which you decide what is right or wrong). But to do so, you must be prepared in both areas of your career: You must develop good technical skills and good human relations.

Playing the Success Game

Many successful people seem to have excellent personalities. That is, they are good at human relations. There is something about them that makes you like them for their own sake.

They get along well with others. But not all famous or successful people are sweet and kind. Many of them do things that offend others, as newspapers and television report almost daily. Some successful people even seem to have bad human relations, though these are few. They must have exceptional talent to get away with it. In such cases, people respect their talent but dislike their personalities at the same time.

Many famous sports figures and show business celebrities seem to go out of their way to offend. And they get away with poor human relations—up to a point. But there is a certain amount of acting in what they do. Their irritating ways are sometimes something of a put-on. They know that their actions will get them publicity and recognition, and they have ability and skill to back them up.

Even so, they have to be careful. In fact, they are fully aware of how to handle human relations. They know just how to play the game in order to be successful. You might say that such people fully understand the important relationship between technical skills and human relations. They get along by making it a point not to go along.

Winning with Human Relations

That you can get along without going along can be seen clearly in the career of Muhammad Ali:

Muhammad Ali proved his talent as a professional boxer again and again. And while he fought for money inside the ring he fought for his beliefs outside it. He refused to fight in a war he did not support— the Vietnam War. As a result, he was sentenced to jail. His title as heavyweight champion of the world—which he had fought hard for and had won fairly in the ring—

was taken from him. But Ali continued to fight. He fought his jail sentence in the courts and won. Yet his beliefs cost him a lot. He was not allowed to box during some of the best years of his life. Even so, he eventually returned to the ring and won his title back.

Muhammad Ali's success was based on more than his unusual talent and skill as a boxer. He also understood human relations. He knew how to handle people with his words and thoughts as well as with his fists. And he never seemed to forget that he had to deal with people outside the ring as well as in it. He added human relations skills to his talent, and his success followed.

Recognizing Human Relations Problems

One way to see the importance of good human relations is to think of people you would rather not be with. In asking yourself why you feel as you do, you will see how much is involved in human relations. Other people's talk, dress, mannerisms, and attitudes may bother you. Your human relations may be spoiled by a habit of yours that you are unaware of but that annoys others. Sometimes a very small habit can turn someone off.

To get an idea of how many factors affect human relations, read the advice column in your local newspaper, such as "Dear Abby," "Ask Beth," or "Miss Manners." Most of the letters are about

Dear Cindy:

After my mother came home from the hospital, we did not discuss her operation with anyone outside the family. But a few days later, it seemed that everyone knew all about it. I finally traced the story to our doctor's assistant. How can I make sure that my medical matters are kept confidential in the future?

Annoyed

Dear Cindy:

My problem is a man who works with me. He is always "borrowing" money—and he never pays me back! When I remind him about it, he laughs it off. I'd like to talk to the boss about it, but this man has been around longer than I have and I'm afraid I'll look like a troublemaker. Would you tell the boss or try to ignore it?

Out Of Money

Dear Cindy:

Alice, who shares my office, seemed nice enough at first. But lately she's stayed out longer and longer at lunch and is coming in later in the morning. I'm doing more than my share of the work and covering up—but I'm getting sick of it. Should I tell my boss about it, or wait until she wakes up and notices it herself?

I don't want to get Alice in trouble—I just want her to do her job!

Had It

poor human relations. People want advice about how to deal with friends, relatives, and co-workers. Their problems range from how people dress or talk to how they behave.

Writers of letters in advice columns, such as the samples on this page, mostly are concerned about human relations problems and these problems are often in the work place.

Human relations involves communication, which is more than making yourself understood. You have to make the person you are talking with want to listen and understand. If you have an annoying habit, you may turn the other person off. For instance, how do you feel about someone who says "you know" or "understand" or "say" or "like" after every phrase? How do you feel about someone who is never on time? Such habits can be seen in others around you. If someone annoys you, try to figure out what the trouble is. Take a look at your own actions in light of what you find annoying in others. In this way, you can improve your own skill at human relations.

Human Relations and Your Career

What does all this have to do with being successful in your career? Well, as you have read, the ability to do the job is usually not enough to ensure success. Often, a career requires that there be no separation between human relations skills and job skills. Both are needed all the time. Salespeople, for example, must have good human relations skills. If they cannot deal with people, they cannot do their job. The skills needed for success as a salesperson are almost entirely human relations skills.

There are many jobs in which dealing with people is important. In such cases, the importance of human relations skills is obvious. Receptionists usually must have typing skills as well as other clerical skills. Often they must operate a switchboard. But no receptionist is successful without an ability to deal with people. This is true no matter how well developed the other skills are.

Teachers, bus drivers, police officers—those whose jobs put them into frequent contact with people—must have good human relations skills. Okay, you may say, that point is obvious. But what about the thousands of jobs in which you do not have to meet people.

All Jobs Require Human Relations

Few, if any, jobs have no contact with people. There may be exceptions. But even the night guard in an office building has contact with people. If the contact is not with the general public, it is with fellow workers and supervisors. You are going to be a plumber? Well, you will have to deal with customers. And you may work with a helper or partner. The same is true if you are a television or appliance repairer.

A truck driver? Although separated physically within the cab of the truck, you still will have to deal with people. And not all human relations is carried out by talking. In fact, an understanding of human relations will help you be a safer driver. For example, a person whose car begins to skid on an icy road will often react by slamming on the brakes, thus aggravating the situation. Recognizing such tendencies—both

in yourself and in others—can help you to avoid accidents.

When you are aware that certain things annoy you, you can try to avoid them or prepare yourself to deal calmly with them. A calm driver is safer than an angry one. Understanding yourself is part of good human relations. In this sense, all careers involve human relations.

Relationships Matter

"Enough of this," you might think. "I'm not going to do any of these things. I'm working on an assembly line. I know my job. It has no contact with people. Well, just a little with the people on either side of me. We just sit there and do our job. We don't have to be experts."

But does a job on an assembly line offer no contact with people? What about contact with your supervisor? What about coffee breaks, lunch hour, getting to work, and going home? You can avoid people during these periods, but you will not be happy if you do. And you probably will not be promoted to supervisor or to other responsible positions that require you to make contact with people. Your unwillingness to do so would make you a poor candidate for promotion.

You Cannot Escape Human Relations

Say, for the sake of the discussion, that you do not care about being promoted. You are an extreme case, and you do not even join other workers during breaks. Are you then free of the need to consider human relations? Unless you are shut off in a room by yourself and can get to and

Certain types of behavior can negatively affect your human relations at work. Studies have shown that if you want to get along well with others, you should avoid annoying behaviors that interfere with your communication with others. If you display some of these behaviors, your working relationships will suffer. Indeed, if you do these things outside of work as well, *all* your relationships will suffer. Here is a list of habits that studies have identified as especially annoying to co-workers. As you review the list, try to see if any of the descriptions could be applied to you.

Being bossy	Looking glum
Backslapping	Losing temper
Bragging	Nosiness
Cheating in games	Overusing slang
Coaxing	Petty lying
Continually criticizing	Pushing to front of lines
Coughing on others	Putting on airs
Cracking gum	Seeking attention
Disrespecting the elderly	Sniffling
Dominating conversations	Spitting
Giving unasked-for advice	Talking about sex
Gossiping	Talking too loudly
Gushing	Trying to be funny
Having body odor or bad	Using baby talk
breath	Using endearing names
Hurrying others	Using high-pressure selling

from that room without seeing anyone, the answer is no.

Say you are working on an assembly line. The worker next to you keeps coughing in your direction. You have a human relations problem to deal with. If *you* are doing the coughing, your neighbor will draw you into a human relations situation.

Perhaps the worker next to you chews gum and keeps cracking it. That can be irritating. Or maybe the worker near you does not take baths regularly or has bad

breath. That could make you and others on the job uncomfortable.

Human relations is an important part of all jobs. And everything you do or do not do affects your human relations. If you do not bathe regularly, if you are late, if you are unpleasant to be around, you will have poor human relations.

Getting along with people—human relations—is important in your career, whatever it is. In the following chapters, you will discover some ways to help you improve your human relations.

Name _____   Date _____

Check Your Understanding

1. It now should be obvious that good human relations skills, or getting along with people, is an important part of success on any job. Below is a list of occupations. If your career interest is not on the list, add it. Then talk with people who are holding these jobs and imagine yourself in each situation. Or use the library to find out more about the work involved. In the columns on the right, place a check mark to show what kind of people each worker will have contact with. After you have completed the exercise, compare your answers with those in the answer key on the last page of this chapter.

	Occupation	Customers	Co-Workers	Supervisors	People to Supervise	Others
a.	Travel agent					
b.	Legal secretary					
c.	Hairdresser					
d.	Office manager					
e.	Electrician					
f.	Telemarketer					
g.	Waiter					
h.	Welder					
i.	Aerobics instructor					
j.	Chef					
k.	Accountant					
l.	Teacher					
m.	Dental assistant					
n.	Hotel housekeeper					
o.	Your career interest					

2. Give an example of how poor human relations can hinder someone in each of these jobs.

a. Travel agent _____

    _____

b. Legal secretary _____

    _____

c. Hairdresser _____

    _____

d. Office manager_____

_____

e. Electrician _____

_____

f. Telemarketer_____

_____

g. Waiter_____

_____

h. Welder _____

_____

i. Aerobics instructor _____

_____

j. Chef_____

_____

k. Accountant_____

_____

l. Teacher _____

_____

m. Dental assistant _____

_____

n. Hotel housekeeper _____

_____

o. Your career interest _____

_____

Case Study

In the situation below, there is a human relations problem. Read about it and then answer the questions to solve the problem. Write your answers in the space provided.

Brian was a talented young artist. Although he had not been out of school long, he had already won awards and prizes in graphic design, drawing, and painting. All through school he had won praise for his designs and illustrations for school publications and posters and for the pictures that he displayed. Now Brian was working for a well-known advertising agency. He had been hired because of his unusual talent, even though he was younger than most of the agency's employees and had less experience. Brian was pleased and proud to have landed a job with such prestige. In fact, he was somewhat conceited about it.

Name _____   *Date* _____

Brian did not consider it necessary to try to get along with his co-workers at the agency. After all, with his talent, who needed other people? He was not rude, but he often failed to greet people he met. He made no effort to learn anyone's name. He expected special attention and recognition for his work and was upset if he did not receive it. Furthermore, he had annoying personal habits. For instance, he constantly combed his hair in public. He would comb it over and over while he sat thinking at his drawing table, scattering loose hairs around as he did so.

Finally Tonesha, who worked next to Brian, mildly complained to him. Brian told her off: "Do you think anyone cared about when or where Michelangelo combed his hair? You're just jealous because I have as good a job as you do at half your age." At this, Tonesha lost her mild manner and complained to her supervisor. The supervisor called Brian in and informed him that several employees had complained about him.

"You do good work, Brian," said the supervisor, "but Michelangelo you're not—at least not yet. I think you should know something about the accomplishments of the other artists." The supervisor showed Brian newspaper clippings about prizes, awards, and praise from critics for the work of Tonesha and others. The supervisor finished by saying, "We'll let this pass this time, Brian, and chalk it up to inexperience. Don't let it happen again."

Case Study Analysis

a. What is the real problem?

_____

_____

b. What are the important facts to consider in this problem?_____

_____

_____

_____

c. What solutions to this problem can you think of? Describe a few. _____

_____

_____

_____

d. What would happen if the solutions you suggested were followed? Explain the results of each solution you described._____

_____

_____

_____

e. Of the solutions you described, which would you recommend? Why?_____

_____

_____

_____

Personal Assessment

To recognize the importance of good human relations on the job, make a comparison of two famous people. Do this by answering the following questions. If possible, do some research, referring to biographies or autobiographies, to support your opinions.

a. Name one famous person who seems to you to have good human relations.

_____

1. What talent makes this person famous?_____

2. Do you like or dislike this person? Why? _____

_____

3. What public image does this person try to present?_____

4. How does this person display good human relations? _____

5. How much is this person's success based on human relations?_____

b. Name one famous person who seems to you to have bad human relations.

_____

1. What talent makes this person famous?_____

2. Do you like or dislike this person? Why? _____

_____

3. What public image does this person try to present?_____

4. How does this person display bad human relations? _____

5. How much is this person's success based on human relations?_____

_____

Answers to Check Your Understanding: 1. a. Customers, co-workers, supervisors; b. Customers, co-workers, supervisors; c. Customers, co-workers, supervisors; d. Co-workers, supervisors, people to supervise, others; e. Customers, co-workers, supervisors; f. Customers, co-workers, supervisors; g. Customers, co-workers, supervisors; h. Co-workers, supervisors; i. Customers, co-workers, supervisors; j. Co-workers, supervisors, people to supervise, others; k. Customers, co-workers, supervisors, people to supervise; l. Co-workers, supervisors, people to supervise (students),   others (parents); m. Customers, co-workers, supervisors; n.Customers, co-workers, supervisors; o.Answers will vary.

Chapter 2

DEVELOPING SELF-AWARENESS

After completing this chapter, you will be able to:

> ➤ *Assess your actions in terms of the five basic needs.*

> ➤ *Recognize the three aspects of character.*

To have good human relations, you must understand people. And the first person you must understand is yourself. You must be aware of yourself. *Self-awareness* does not mean being *self-conscious* or being selfish. A self-conscious or selfish person usually has poor human relations. If you are self-conscious or selfish, you may be too busy thinking only about yourself to relate well to other people. Self-awareness is a different thing, as this case shows:

Peter was self-conscious without being truly aware of himself. He was quite handsome and, when he was at ease, he had a nice smile and a good speaking voice. But unfortunately for Peter, he was seldom at ease among other people. He was too busy thinking about himself and wondering how he looked to others.

"Is my shirt in? How's my hair? Did I say that word right? Should I have stood up? Should I sit down?" All these questions and more would be running through Peter's head all the time. His face would freeze, and his voice would become strained. If he had been aware of his many good points and less self-conscious about what kind of an impression he was making, he would easily have made a very good impression. As it was, he did not.

When you lack a self-identity, that is, you do not understand yourself—you tend to be impatient, lazy, and restless. You are unable to stick to anything for long. You are, in fact, a self-conscious person who is too busy agonizing about yourself to really learn about yourself or to pay much attention to others. You cannot build good human relations if you are like this.

You Must Like Yourself to Like Others

A *self-identity* is important because you must know yourself in order to develop a sense of purpose. Out of your values and your sense of purpose, you develop your *self-esteem* or sense of worth—a liking and a respect for yourself.

Now you may have heard many times that it is conceited or somehow bad to like yourself. This is not true. It is good—it is essential—for you to like yourself. In fact, you first must like yourself before you can begin liking others. Although you can have polite relations with someone you do not care for, it is easier to have good relations with people for whom you do care. If you do not care for yourself, if you have no self-esteem, you will have poor human relations because you will not be able to care about anyone else.

First of all, then, you need a healthy liking for yourself. That does not mean you should stand admiring yourself in front of a mirror. It means having a healthy liking in which you can see both your good points and your bad points without false humility or excessive pride.

If you are able to look at yourself without ignoring or enlarging either your good or your bad points, you probably have the self-confidence to deal easily with other people. Think about that for a moment. Knowing other people is important. But the most important thing is to know yourself first. With that knowledge, you will have the strength to deal with all kinds of people in all kinds of situations. Self-knowledge is the basis for good human relations.

Be Aware of Your Needs and Others'

To understand yourself—and others—it is helpful to know that all people have certain *needs* and that, in general, they spend their lives fulfilling these needs.

Human needs have been classified into five general types. Experts on how people behave say that these needs can be arranged in the order in which people seek to satisfy them. These needs and the order in which everyone meets them are:

1. The need to keep alive

2. The need to be free of fear and anxiety

3. The need to be loved

4. The need to be admired and respected

5. The need to realize your potential

The first involves your *physical needs*, the others your *psychological needs*. The basic motivation for all your actions stems from these five general needs. Sometimes you strive to satisfy more than one need at a time. But you must always satisfy the first need before you can go on to the second, and so on. A closer look at these five human needs follows.

The Need to Keep Alive

If you cannot keep yourself alive, obviously you cannot satisfy any other needs. Keeping yourself alive requires eating and breathing and taking care of your body functions. Some of these things, such as breathing, you do automatically, or without conscious effort. You are forced to do other things by demands your body makes, although you can control the demands to some extent. You can put off eating when you first feel hunger—at least for a while. But you will have to eat sometime to stay alive.

The Need to be Free of Fear and Anxiety

Once you have done what is necessary to keep alive, you want to make yourself as safe and as comfortable as possible. You dress to keep warm and dry. You try to avoid obvious physical dangers. The unknown can threaten you, and so you try to organize your life. You set up daily routines and habits. You try to change people or situations that make you feel insecure, and you surround yourself with people and situations that make you feel safe.

The Need to be Loved

You meet your need for love and affection in many ways. Research shows that babies who are raised without care and love may develop into normal adults physically, but their human relations will suffer because they have not learned how to give or get affection. Children learn from their families and friends how to behave in order to get love. Later, as adults, they still seek love through marriage, through being generous, and in other ways. You never outgrow the need to have others treat you with affection, care, and love.

The decision to love somebody is *not* simply a sexual attraction. It is a commitment to another person. You hope to share happy moments together. But when there are sad moments and disappointments, you stand by the ones you love. This need to give and receive love makes you join clubs and groups, ties you to your family, and makes you seek out and please friends. You want to feel that you belong.

The Need to be Admired and Respected

Once you feel that you belong, that people like you, you then want them to respect you. This is particularly true of your peer group. You want to earn their admiration as well as their love. You need admiration and attention, which build your self-esteem. In school, you seek the approval of your teachers by doing well. On the job, you try to please your bosses or supervisors so that they will show approval. This ties in with your need to stay alive, because a boss's approval often takes the form of a pay raise, which will buy food, shelter, and so on.

The Need to Realize Your Potential

All people have a sense of what they can do and achieve in life. When your other needs are taken care of, you can think of what you are capable of doing. But you do more than just think about it. You try to fulfill yourself by doing what you know you can. If you do not fulfill yourself in this way, you become frustrated.

Realizing your potential in this sense does *not* simply mean becoming rich or famous or powerful. Those things may be involved, but a person who earns a living by growing flowers may be happier and more fulfilled than one who is rich and powerful. Fulfillment depends upon how you feel about what you are doing. If you know you can do more, the need for self-fulfillment will make you try to do so. Until you have explored your full potential, you will not feel fulfilled.

To satisfy this final need, you first must have a realistic idea of your potential. Most people do. But consider whether you underestimate or overestimate your potential. If you underestimate yourself, you will be satisfied too easily and will make excuses for yourself. You will avoid challenges and will never learn all you are capable of. If you overestimate yourself, you will feel frustrated because you cannot achieve what you think you can. People who always fail to reach their goal should try to set more realistic goals.

Your idea of what you can achieve will change through life. It can change as the result of reevaluation. At one time, you may have thought that earning good grades was not very important. Then you realized that your school record could help you get the job you wanted. You reevaluated what was important, and you saw that you could get higher grades with just a little effort.

Your evaluation of yourself can also change as a result of recognition, as Don's did:

Don always got high grades in math, but he never seemed to do well in English class. One day, he was asked to read one of his papers out loud to the class. He was praised by the teacher and by his classmates for work well done. Don had never thought of himself as a good writer.

But from that day on, Don realized that he had the potential to improve upon his writing skills, and he saw that the effort would pay off. Until then, he had avoided thinking about any career that included writing. Now Don's potential was greater because others had recognized a talent he had overlooked in himself.

Your idea of what you can do may also change as a result of actual achievement. You may set an early goal to become a supervisor in the factory where you work. After becoming a supervisor, you may realize that you have the ability to be a general manager. Thus, you begin to work to achieve that position.

Needs and Human Relations

When you know yourself and what motivates you, you are better able to get along with others. On a simple level, you may know that when you are hungry, you tend to become annoyed. With that understanding, you would be wise to avoid situations in which you might be dealing with people on sensitive matters when you are hungry. Many people in business prefer to talk about things like contract negotiations either at lunch or just after lunch.

As your needs are met, you will become more relaxed and agreeable. When they are not met, you may become tense and disagreeable. Your mood influences your human relations. You cannot help it. But you can control it.

In short, meeting your needs makes it easy to maintain good human relations. And good human relations makes it easier to meet your needs. This cycle is

further proof of what you learned in the first chapter: People are social animals, and no one works alone.

Becoming Aware of Your Character

Do you realize that there are three aspects to your character? These have been created and shaped by your experiences. In any given situation, one or another of these aspects might be strongest. In some people, one part may be stronger than the other two. But it is best when all three are balanced.

For simplicity, experts have labeled these three aspects of character the *"adult,"* the *"parent,"* and the *"child."* When these ordinary words are used in this way, they relate only slightly to what is usually meant by an adult, a parent, or a child. But your character aspects are similar to these three different groups. At some time, and to some degree, the adult, parent, and child aspects come out.

The Parent in You

The parent part of your character is made up of the rules and teachings that you absorbed at an early age. Since you got most of these ideas from your parents and since you use them as a parent does toward a small child, "parent" is an appropriate term to describe this particular aspect of your character.

As the parent, you may try to give orders, be overbearing, or act intimidating. This part of your character makes you critical of others. It is the parent acting in you who unthinkingly says that something is good or bad. Your prejudices are found in your parent self. Some things in your parent self are good. They are automatic and stem from common sense. They can be life-saving commands, such as "Don't play with a loaded gun!"

When this aspect of character is in command of a human relations situation, you act mostly in an unthinking manner. You rely on the basic ideas you learned when you were young, without testing to see whether they suit the occasion.

The Child in You

If the parent part of your character reflects your preconceived thoughts and ideas, the child part reflects your emotions. And when the child takes control, you act out these emotions. This can be good when your feelings are happy. It is not so good when you have sad, angry, or mean feelings.

As the term suggests, the child self wants someone else to take control and say what to do. It even wants to be criticized. When the child aspect of your character takes control, you want to follow others rather than to lead or be active. But the child self is not all negative or passive. It also carries the urge to be creative.

The Adult in You

The adult is the questioning aspect of your character. When the adult is in control, you do not respond only with a preconceived idea or with emotion. Instead, you consider all the facts before you. You shift through the responses available in the child self and in the parent self. You then pick the right response. If you are dealing with a loaded gun, the right response is the parental command, "Don't play with a loaded gun!" The child response is not so good: "Let's shoot it to hear the bang!"

The adult self represents a thinking response to a situation rather than the more automatic responses of the child self or the parent self. After thinking the situation over, you may call upon the child self or the parent self to respond. You may even use a combination of the two if the adult self is in control.

Character and Human Relations

Good human relations usually will result if you develop the adult self and let this aspect of character control you. Certainly, in most situations, it is best to think before you act.

Sometimes, though, the automatic reaction of the child self or the parent self is more suitable. If you always take time to think, you may earn a reputation for being cold or distant. If you are like that, or even if people think you are, it will be difficult to develop warm, easy relations with others.

Although most people react automatically much of the time, their reactions are not always the most suitable ones. You should consider yourself lucky if your automatic response is usually the right one. If it is not, you can work to correct it. By identifying the different aspects of yourself, you can usually tell if an undesirable part is too strong. Once you learn that, you can correct it. All people react with different aspects of their character from time to time. There is no harm in that. But sometimes that reaction is useful, and sometimes it is not.

Human relations problems develop when you act or react in one way only. If you have had to put up with a bossy person who is always acting out the parent self, you know how unpleasant it is to deal with such a person. On the other hand, dealing with people who can only display the child, who always want support, is also annoying.

If you wonder whether one aspect of your character is too strong, ask yourself this question: "What behavior do I find most annoying in other people?" Then think about the answer. It is often true—though not always—that the behavior trait you find most annoying in others is one you yourself exhibit.

Self-Awareness Not Self-Absorption

Being *self-aware* is having an honest perception of yourself that balances your good and bad points. Being *self-absorbed* means you are concentrating so much on imagined characteristics of yourself, you have no room for reality. You can become too self-conscious in trying to become more self-aware.

Try to avoid this, but do think about yourself from time to time and evaluate what you do.

This self-evaluation is important after you have made an error or failed to accomplish a goal. But do not spend too much time on yourself.

Today there are many experts studying people and how they behave, and many television commercials, advertisements, and other pressures to be a certain way. It is possible to think about and examine yourself too much.

There is an ancient myth about a young man named Narcissus who became so absorbed in examining himself that he lost interest in everything and everybody else. All he did was stare at his own reflection in a pond.

Those who fall in love with themselves as Narcissus did will not be able to meet their human needs because they will fail at human relations.

Name _____   Date _____

Check Your Understanding

If you can understand yourself, you can strengthen your good points and improve upon your weaknesses. One way to gain self-awareness is to recognize when the parent, child, and adult parts of your character are in control. Sometimes watching these traits at work in other people can help you to see them in yourself.

Read the statements below. Decide whether you think the person is displaying the parent, child, or adult aspect of her or his character. Then place a check mark in the appropriate column on the right. After you have completed the exercise, compare your answers with those in the answer key on the last page of this chapter.

		Parent	*Child*	*Adult*
a.	"I know the party next Saturday is going to be rowdy and things will get out of control. So I've decided not to go."			
b.	"Actually, Juanita, I don't know whether you should go out with Bob. Lisamarie had a bad experience with him."			
c.	When the teacher announced the homework assignment, Jack looked at his classmate, Rene, raised his eyebrows, and gave a sigh.			
d.	"Can I help you? I used that kind of computer in one of my courses last year."			
e.	"If you do not play it my way, I'm not going to play."			
f.	Pedro said to Angie, "Don't lie! You should have been working on this yesterday."			
g.	"Don't eat so much of that greasy food. It's not good for you."			
h.	"I think everyone is different. I mean, you can't really say that all people in one group are just alike."			
i.	"I'm not sure I can do this job. Please watch how I'm doing and help me when it gets busy."			
j.	"I don't want to do this exercise. I'd rather rent a movie."			

Case Study

In the situation below, there is a human relations problem. Read about it and then answer the questions to solve the problem. Write your answers in the space provided.

Nan worked as a lab assistant at a large chemical firm. She liked her job but she did not like wearing a lab coat when working with chemicals. She was very conscious of her appearance. She wore the very latest styles all the time. She spent hours getting her hair just right and putting on makeup. Whenever she saw some new cosmetic advertised on television, she would hurry to buy it and try it out.

As a result, Nan was always broke. All her money was spent on clothes and cosmetics to make her more attractive. Also, she was always too busy making herself up and dressing to do anything else. She was almost always late for social engagements. She also was often late for work. Twice Nan passed up promotions, once because she would have had to wear a face mask and cap for safety reasons, which she thought would mess up her makeup and hair. On rainy days, Nan sometimes called in sick to avoid getting her hair wet and having it look messy and straggly at work.

Nan always wore the best clothes she could buy. Although she wore a lab coat at work to protect her street clothes, she twice spilled chemicals that ruined expensive pants. Her supervisor suggested that she wear less-expensive clothes to work. But Nan felt she had to look her best all the time. She was sure everyone would notice even the smallest thing wrong with an outfit she wore.

Case Study Analysis

a. What is the real problem?_____

_____

_____

_____

b. What are the important facts to consider in this problem?_____

_____

_____

_____

_____

c. What solutions to this problem can you think of? Describe a few. _____

_____

_____

_____

_____

d. What would happen if the solutions you suggested were followed? Explain the results of each solution you described._____

_____

_____

_____

_____

e. Of the solutions you described, which would you recommend? Why? _____

_____

_____

_____

_____

Name _____   Date _____

Personal Assessment

It is helpful in building good human relations to know which of the five needs you are satisfying when you do something. In the left-hand column of the chart below, make a list of all the things you did and the decisions you made yesterday. Analyze each activity in terms of the five general needs you are meeting, either directly or indirectly. Then place a check mark in the appropriate column(s) on the right. For example, by eating, you satisfy the first need of keeping alive. Maybe you skipped breakfast because, at the moment, your need for food was not as great as some other need. By studying, you may satisfy several needs. You could be trying to avoid fear and anxiety that you might feel when you do not have your work done. Or you could be seeking appreciation by doing something that you know will please your parents or teachers.

You may not be able to identify all your actions in terms of your needs, but try to do so. Discuss the ones you are not sure of with your classmates.

Activity	To Keep Alive	To Be Free of Fear/ Anxiety	To Be Loved	To Be Admired, Respected	To Realize Potential

Activity	To Keep Alive	To Be Free of Fear/ Anxiety	To Be Loved	To Be Admired, Respected	To Realize Potential

Answers to Check Your Understanding: a. Adult; b. Adult; c. Child; d. Adult; e. Child; f. Parent; g. Parent; h. Adult; i. Child; j. Child.

Chapter **3**

THE FORCES THAT SHAPE YOU

After completing this chapter, you will be able to:

➤ *Recognize the role of genes in determining personality and physical characteristics.*

➤ *Recognize the role of environment in determining personality and behaviors.*

➤ *Identify the four different environments that help shape you.*

GENETIC INFLUENCES

People in a family often look alike, sound alike, even walk alike.

- Do you look like your mother or father, or one of your grandparents?

- Do people who hear your voice over the phone think you are your brother or sister?

- Do people in your family ever say you remind them of a particular aunt or uncle?

People in the same family often share similar physical traits and behavioral characteristics. You inherit these characteristics from your parents, who inherited their characteristics from their parents.

For centuries, people have known that traits are passed from parent to child. Farmers observed that the seed from the healthiest plants produced the best crops. Animal breeders saw that the offspring of even-tempered animals were also even-tempered. Cows who were good milk-producers gave birth to cows that were also productive.

If you are planning to buy a puppy or kitten, you want to see or know about the mother and father. If they are friendly and calm, you are more apt to buy the animal than if they are aggressive or nervous. If they are healthy, with clear coats and good bone structure, you feel confident that their offspring are healthy as well.

Genetic Characteristics

In the 1800s, Gregor Mendel, an Austrian monk, discovered that by crossbreeding pea plants, he could produce plants that had certain characteristics. He discovered that parents carried certain elements—called genes—which they transferred to their offspring.

Mendel proved that the combination of genes from both parents determined the characteristics of the offspring.

The combination of genes you inherit plays a role in determining your personal characteristics. This *genetic inheritance* affects both your appearance—your physical characteristics—and your behavior. Take the example of Justin.

Justin was the middle son in his family. His older brother and his younger brother both looked like their mother. But Justin looked like his father. When he saw pictures of his father as a boy, he thought he was looking at pictures of himself. Justin's mother and his brothers had dark hair and hazel eyes, while Justin and his father were blond with brown eyes.

People were always saying how much Justin and his father were alike. They both had artistic talent and liked science. Justin went to art school, like his father. But Justin was not exactly like his father. His father was quiet, almost shy, and never lost his temper. Justin was outgoing and gregarious, like his mother, and like her, he became angry quickly. People who knew

Justin well knew that, although he looked like his dad, his personality was a combination of both his parents' personalities.

Genes Influence Behavior

The genes you inherit from your parents carry a genetic code—the instructions for producing the enzymes and other proteins that are important to the development of all your body's organ systems. The functioning of these body systems— your brain and nervous system, musculoskeletal, digestive, excretory, respiratory, cardiovascular, and glandular systems—affects your behavior.

How can genes influence behavior? By directly influencing certain physical characteristics and body functions, genes have an indirect effect on behavior. For example, studies have indicated that a person can inherit a tendency toward shyness or toward being an extrovert. Also, aspects of a person's physical structure—being tall or short, dark or light, large or small—are influenced by inherited genes and these physical characteristics can have a bearing on a person's behavior.

Your Potential

You inherited a variety of potentials. Potential is a range of capacity for growth. This range, which can be large or small, is determined by the genes you inherited from your parents. In some areas, you inherited a small range of potential. Your genetic inheritance limits the range of choices for such physical characteristics as eye, hair, and skin color, height, and body type. Scientists agree that these traits are inherited because the range or difference between parent and child is usually small.

A large potential range between parent and child is evident in many behavior characteristics. Talents, skills, food preferences, and other characteristics are not as clearly affected by genetic inheritance. Environment plays a large role in the development of these traits.

Is someone a talented artist because he or she inherited that talent from a parent who is also artistic? Or possibly because good eye-hand coordination was inherited? Or is it because the home environment encouraged the development of artistic talent? The answer might be that all three factors are important.

ENVIRONMENTAL INFLUENCES

Genes do not operate alone. As you trace the pathway from genes to behavior, you must take the *environmental influence* into account. Environment influences the parent of the child and the child from earliest development to adulthood. Environment can also alter the genetic inheritance of the child in cases where the parent has been exposed to certain harmful substances or phenomena, such as radiation.

Different kinds of environments influence you in different ways. These different environments are:

- physical environment,

- cultural environment,

- social environment, and

- internal environment.

Your Physical Environment

Your physical environment refers to your physical or material surroundings. Do you live under crowded conditions or in isolation? Are you surrounded by noise or by silence? Are your surroundings boring or stimulating?

What is the climate like where you live, and how does that influence your surroundings? Is your physical environment healthy, or are you exposed to dangerous or polluted conditions? These are some of the aspects of physical environment. Each particular aspect influences behavior.

Your Cultural Environment

Your cultural environment refers to the system of ways of behaving in your community. Your cultural environment shapes your behavior. You act in certain ways because those are the ways that are approved of by your community. What is normal behavior in one culture may be abnormal in another.

Customs are the accepted ways of behavior in a community. Many laws are based upon customs. Etiquette, being polite and courteous to others, is a system of customs that influences behavior in society.

Different communities have different cultural values. These cultural values define what is and is not important in a society. For example, American society, in general, values education and material success.

Your Social Environment

Your social environment refers to the people you have contact with. Your family is your first social environment, and their influence on your behavior and your personality is great. You first learned how to behave by imitating the behavior of your family.

Feedback from the people in your social environment helps to shape your self-concept. You form your self-concept from the reactions of others. Your motives, values, interests, needs, wants, desires, and aspirations are all influenced by your self-concept. Look at the way that Janey's environment influenced her.

Janey came from a poor family. They lived in a crowded and noisy apartment building. Janey did not feel deprived, however, because her friends lived in the same conditions. In addition, her family was a strong, loving one. Her grandparents lived with them and took care of Janey and her sisters while their parents worked. Janey was always aware of being surrounded by people who loved and cared for her.

Janey's parents encouraged her efforts to get good grades. They impressed on her the importance of a good education. They wanted her to graduate from high school, and to be the first person in her family to attend college. They worked and saved to help pay for her education after high school.

Some of her friends were not as lucky. Their families found it harder to show love and support for them. In some cases, the parents worked all the time, and they were too tired to give their children the support and guidance they needed. In others, the parents had given up; the poverty of their neighborhood and the conditions they lived under had left them feeling hopeless.

Janey's friends did not feel that an education was such an important thing. On nice days, they skipped school and tried to convince Janey to join them. They sometimes called her a "brain" and a "grind" because of the good grades she got.

Janey knew that she was no smarter than they were; she just worked harder. School was her first priority.

Your Internal Environment

The last environment that is important in shaping your behavior is literally within your skin—your internal environment. One aspect of your internal environment is your biochemical environment.

Hormonal changes and drugs can affect your moods and temperament. Your mental state can, in turn, affect your body. You can actually increase or decrease your heartbeat and blood pressure, for example, through the technique of biofeedback.

Heredity and environment act together to influence your behavior. You can see that you are a unique individual because of the combination of your genes and your environment.

PERSONALITY

The unique characteristics that identify you as an individual form your personality. Al-

though you may resemble your parents and siblings, you are not just like them. You are unique. Your personality is one of the unique things about you. Even identical twins, who have the same genes and are usually raised in the same environment, have different personalities.

While we are all alike in some respects, none of us are alike in all respects. Some of the basic characteristics often used to describe personality are the following:

* masculinity/feminity

* shyness/outgoingness

* flexibility/rigidity

* dominance/submissiveness

* people orientation/thing orientation

* initiating action/responding to external control

While you can do very little to change your genes, you can change both your environment and your personality. As you read this book, you will get a better understanding of your personality. As a result, you may identify certain aspects of your personality that you would like to change. Do not expect to make radical changes. Often, small changes have a tremendous effect on how other people relate to you, and your degree of success in achieving your goals.

You are interacting with your environment even before you are born. In the womb, you take what you need from the environment—oxygen and nutrients—and react to things that happen—loud noises and cigarette smoke. Prenatal lead poisoning or exposure to alcohol and other drugs can have a lasting effect on a person.

Your Environment and Genes Influence Your Personality

Many theories have been put forth to explain personality, why there are different types, and how each one develops. Although there are no simple explanations, it is safe to say that the combined influences of your environment and your genes effect your personality.

Because of your type of personality, you are inclined to act certain ways in certain situations.

A child who talks early and clearly may grow up to be someone who loves to talk. If that child was encouraged by his or her family to talk, was listened to and given positive feedback, he or she may grow up to enjoy speaking in public, and have an outgoing personality.

If another child, also with good verbal ability, grows up in a family that believes "children should be seen and not heard," he or she may have turned to writing as a form of expression, and be a quiet and private person.

Your Skills Are Part of Your Personality

Skills are one component of your personality. These include motor skills, such as walking, running, skipping, writing, carving, and drawing; and learning skills, such as remembering, reasoning, and sensing.

Learning skills are also called cognitive skills. A skill can be done more than once and has a specific beginning and an end.

There are so many skills that even scientists have not tried to count them all. The very lowest levels of skills are called abilities. For example, good hand-eye coordination is an ability that may help you learn many skills—typing, woodworking, sewing, tennis, drafting. Good hand-eye coordination is not enough, however, without training in a particular skill.

Name _____   Date _____

Check Your Understanding

Your potential, your behavior, and your personality are all influenced by the four different environments: physical, cultural, social, and internal.

Read the statements below. Which environment is influencing the subject of the statement? Place a check in the appropriate column to the right. After you have completed the exercise, compare your answers with those in the answer key on the last page of this chapter.

		Physical	Cultural	Social	Internal
a.	Caleb arrived at work looking tired. He was not in a good mood. Last night had been very hot. His fan was broken, and through the open windows he heard yelling and shouting from the street. He kept waking up.				
b.	Jeanine knew she should not have that cola drink. The caffeine in it always made her jumpy. Now she was snapping at her co-workers.				
c.	After work, the guys in Alfredo's crew liked to go out on the town. Alfredo never joined them. After working long hours all week, he wanted to get home. He and his wife always had a special dinner on Friday nights.				
d.	Hiroshi's behavior sometimes surprised his American colleagues. He was unfailingly polite, and never argued at business meetings. He nodded his head during presentations as if to say yes. His colleagues thought that he was responding in a positive way to their ideas, and were puzzled when he turned down their proposal.				
e.	Manuel excelled in track and field. His favorite events were the long-distance races. His coaches and teammates counted on his strength and energy to help them win the state championship.				
f.	Patrice felt that fashionable clothing and jewelry were the most important thing for making friends at school. She was one of the "in" group and only bought high-fashion, name-brand jeans and sneakers.				
g.	Annie liked to spend some time at the library at least once every few weeks. Ever since childhood when her mother took her to the library, she had enjoyed reading. She would select two or three new novels each time. Being an avid reader, she always found time to read whether on the train to work or in the evening.				

Case Study

In the situation described below, there is a human relations problem. Read the situation and then answer the questions to solve the problem. Write your answers in the space provided.

Bethany was the third Passarelli girl to enter Bayville High School. Her sister Heather was a senior, and Shawna was a junior. Bethany had looked forward to high school for a long time. She would finally find out what Heather and Shawna had been talking about for so long.

The Passarelli girls were hard to miss—tall, slim, dark-eyed, and with curly dark hair, they all looked exactly like their mother. And they sounded alike, especially on the telephone. Sometimes even their friends had trouble telling who was who from the back or across a room.

Shawna and Heather were popular with their classmates and their friends. Outgoing, vivacious, and athletic, they were both joiners—cheerleaders and volleyball players. Heather was senior class vice-president and Shawna was on the student council. Both girls consistently made the honor roll and were active participants in class discussions. They were the featured vocalists in the glee club, blessed with their father's musical talent.

When the other students and teachers saw another Passarelli girl come, they naturally assumed that Bethany would follow the path of her sisters. But Bethany, while she looked like Shawna and Heather, was very unlike them in temperament and personality. Where they were extroverts, she was shy and introverted. While they enjoyed being the center of attention, Bethany hated the limelight, preferring the company of one or two good friends. Good grades came easily to Heather and Shawna; Bethany had to work hard for her grades, and they were never A's. She was not particularly athletic, and disliked team sports. She preferred bicycling or running to organized games.

When Bethany got a C on her first English exam, the teacher commented that her sisters had never gotten a grade below a B. It was not the last time that teachers compared her to her sisters. They regretted her shyness and told her often how much her sisters contributed to class discussions.

Bethany's most humiliating experience occurred in music class, however. The music teacher, anticipating another Passarelli sister with a beautiful voice, insisted that Bethany sing the solo part one day. She refused to listen to Bethany's statement that she did not have a lovely singing voice like her sisters. Bethany left the classroom in tears.

Bethany began dreading school, which she had looked forward to so eagerly. She started to think that there was something wrong with her because she was not as talented, smart, and outgoing as her sisters.

Name _____   Date _____

Case Study Analysis

a. What is the real problem?_____

_____

_____

_____

_____

b. What are the important facts to consider in this problem?_____

_____

_____

_____

_____

c. What solutions to this problem can you think of? Describe a few. _____

_____

_____

_____

_____

d. What would happen if the solutions you suggested were followed? Explain
the results of each solution you described._____

_____

_____

_____

_____

_____

e. Of the solutions you described, which would you recommend? Why? _____

_____

_____

_____

_____

_____

Personal Assessment

What makes you uniquely you? On a sheet of paper, list everything about yourself that contributes to your makeup. Include physical characteristics, personality traits, abilities, talents, and skills. Imagine that you are describing yourself to someone else through this list of words and phrases. Make your description as complete as possible.

Now go back and decide what factors have contributed to the formation of the person described on your list. Write a G next to those characteristics that were inherited from your parents. Write an E next to the characteristics that were a result of your environment. You may find that some traits—such as mechanical ability—are a combination of both genetic inheritance and your environment.

Answers to Check Your Understanding: a. physical;   b. internal; c. social;   d. cultural; e. internal; f. social; g. social.

Chapter 4

UNDERSTANDING OTHERS

After completing this chapter, you will be able to:

➤ *Identify four keys for understanding others.*

➤ *Assess your effectiveness at understanding others.*

Everyone is different from everyone else, but we all have the same basic ingredients. How these ingredients are mixed in each person makes that person an individual. How they are mixed is determined by heredity (genes) and environmental factors, as you read.

Almost all people have two arms, two legs, one mouth, two eyes, two ears, and so on. But the size, weight, length, color, and shape of these physical traits differ from person to person. Just as a person's physical appearance is made up of the same basic ingredients, so is each person's personality—the nonphysical traits that make one an individual.

When you learn about yourself, you learn something about others as well. Everyone has the same five needs you read of in Chapter 2. Everyone satisfies these needs in the same general order. First, people need to stay alive, then to be free of fear and anxiety, then to be loved, then to be respected, and then to realize their potential.

Knowing that everyone has these needs helps you to understand others. Usually, however, you cannot know which need a person might be responding to. If you are starving, your need for food is obvious. But if you are only hungry, you may postpone satisfying this basic need to meet another need. If you are on a diet, you will resent anyone who forces food on you. That person is not practicing good human relations.

It is difficult—sometimes impossible—to pinpoint exactly which need a person is trying to satisfy at any moment. Everyone's approach to fulfilling needs is a mixture of experience and heredity. Out of this mix, people develop the three aspects of character: the parent self, the child self, and the adult self. We all contain these aspects. The parent self contains the rules and beliefs received at an early age. The child self responds automatically with emotion or creativity and wants someone else to make decisions. The adult self looks for the reality of each situation, asks questions, and responds.

No two people—not even identical twins—have exactly the same mix of experience and heredity. Thus, the three aspects of personality differ in each person. Some individuals will have a strong parent self, others will have a strong adult self, and still others will have a strong child self.

All this is important in human relations. The more you know about people, the better you get along with them. If you have no idea what makes another person tick, you cannot relate well.

Four general points to be aware of to maintain good human relations are:

1. Everyone is unique.

2. Everyone wants to feel important.

3. People have many roles.

4. Needs affect actions.

Use these keys to understanding others and maintain good human relations.

Everyone is Unique

One of the most important things that you can know about anyone is that no two people are alike. Knowing that no two people are alike may seem obvious and of little use. But this knowledge is helpful in maintaining good human relations. If you know this and follow it, you will not make the mistake of grouping people and then treating everyone in a particular group in the same way, or simply treating everyone in the same manner.

This latter mistake is made by people visiting a foreign country, who do not realize that people in the new country might not be like the people back home. Addressing someone by his or her first name, a gesture considered friendly in one country, may be seen as rude in another country. Knowing that everyone is different will keep you from thinking that everyone will behave as you do, or that everyone will react as you do.

You will find people who behave as you do. These people probably will become your friends. But even your closest friends will see some things differently from you. To maintain your friendship, you must recognize and accept this, or make allowances for it. In fact, the closer you are to a person, the more you must be aware of your differences. Assume that you have differences, and look for them. Otherwise, you may find yourself in the spot that Roger and Janet did.

Roger and Janet had been friends since childhood. The two seemed to think alike in everything. For Janet's birthday, Roger wanted to give her a special gift. Roger loved chess and he knew Janet did. He decided the perfect gift for Janet would be a new chess set. He was sure Janet would be thrilled with it. But when Janet opened the present, she just stared and then she mumbled, "Thank you. It's very nice."

"You don't really like it," Roger said.

"Oh, I do," Janet replied. "It's just that I was surprised. You know I've been working all year carving my own chess set out of wood."

"But," said Roger, "I thought you'd be even happier with a real chess set from a store."

Janet and Roger made the best of it. They kept playing chess together. By Janet's birthday, the two friends knew each other better than before. They were aware of their differences as well as their similarities. Roger now understood that Janet liked something she could make for herself. This time, Roger went out and got his friend new carving tools and a box of carving wood.

People are different. If you are unaware that differences exist, you may have bad human relations. But if you learn to respect and appreciate the differences, you will find many friendships.

Everyone Wants to Feel Important

For successful human relations, then, you must recognize that other people are different, and you must respect their differences. It is natural to feel that what is different from you is somehow not as good, or may even be bad.

After all, you know yourself best. But just as you excuse and explain your own actions, you must realize that others have good reasons for their actions too. You must respect their right to be different, just as you expect them to let you do things your own way.

No one likes it when somebody shows that he or she does not respect them. Lack of respect makes a person feel like a nobody. Here is a safe guide to follow in dealing with people: Everyone wants to *feel important*.

Test it on yourself. Think of some time when you felt put down. Maybe a classmate laughed at you for asking a "silly" question. Perhaps a sales clerk ignored you but waited on a customer who came in later. Maybe someone with authority harshly told you to do something.

How did you feel in such situations? Unimportant? Like a nobody? Were you comfortable? Did you enjoy it? Did you want to have much to do with the person who put you down?

Probably you would not want to see someone who put you down and made you feel small—except, perhaps, to get even. Well, assume that others feel the same way. Unless you want to annoy people and make them want to get even, try to show that you respect their right to be special and important.

Think about the five basic human needs. Three of them—being loved, being respected, and realizing your potential—are included in the need to feel important. The only people who do not have this general need are those who have not satisfied the first two needs. Someone who is starving will not be concerned about feeling special and important. Food will be more important. Someone filled with fear for physical safety will not care much about it either.

Usually, however, the people you deal with have satisfied these two basic needs to some extent. They will want to feel important. Your success at human relations will be affected by how well you make other people feel like a somebody and how well you avoid making them feel like a nobody.

This rule applies to all the people you meet. Often it may seem unnecessary to show this concern for those who have authority. But they too have the need to feel liked. In school or on the job, you can let your teachers or supervisors know that you think they are somebody without polishing apples or buttering them up. It is simply a matter of treating others as you would like to be treated. Bill overlooked that fact:

Bill did not intend to seem rude. He just did not see any reason to be friendly with his boss, Ms. Rowbotham. After all, the boss was important because she was the boss. She did not need to be reminded of that by the newest employee. He was also a little in awe of her.

One day, Ms. Rowbotham joined Bill and some other workers during a break. When she started to tell a joke, Bill got up to get another soda. He did not think he was being rude. He told himself that someone as important as Ms. Rowbotham would not even notice that he left. But Ms. Rowbotham did notice. She said nothing, but wondered why Bill was so rude. Fortunately for Bill, an older worker, Olivia, talked to him.

"Ms. Rowbotham's a good person," Olivia told him. "You ought to try to get to know her. It seems that every

time she comes around, you either move or clam up. She's going to think you don't like her."

"She's the boss," Bill said. "What does she care about what I think?"

Bill forgot that everybody—even a boss—wants to feel special. And he did not realize that every person can make someone else feel unimportant by showing that she or he does not respect that person. And Bill made one more mistake: He failed to consider the whole person.

People Play Many Roles

Bill saw Ms. Rowbotham simply as a boss. He did not think of her as a human being with the same needs as everyone else. When you put people into boxes and react to them on only one level, you are practicing poor human relations.

People are not just bosses, or teachers, or parents, or brothers, or sisters, or coworkers. They are other things as well. People fill many roles, which make up the whole person. To have good human relations, you must consider the whole person.

Bernice was an electrician's helper for a construction company. Raoul, the electrician she worked with, was usually fair and pleasant. Lately, though, he was edgy and angry. He shouted at Bernice for no real reason. Often he criticized her unfairly for being slow or careless.

This was hard for Bernice to take. She began to dislike Raoul and to argue with him. Then Bernice learned that

Raoul's child was very ill. She understood that he was a father as well as an electrician. She knew that Raoul's behavior was a result of worrying about his child.

Bernice decided to tolerate Raoul's moods. When the child got well, Raoul became his old self again. He even showed his appreciation to Bernice by telling the boss how helpful she had been.

If Bernice had not taken the whole person into consideration, she might have ended their relationship. Instead, she practiced good human relations. Here's another example:

Walter worked in one division of a large company. His good friend Louise worked in another division. Walter received a promotion and was transferred into Louise's division. Louise had the senior position, and part of Walter's new job was to assist her.

Walter looked forward to working with his friend. But things did not go well. Although there was plenty of work, Louise tried to do it all. She worked during breaks and lunch hours, and stayed late. She did not give Walter much to do. That made him uncomfortable. Sometimes when Louise was out of the office, the boss gave Walter some work. When Louise learned this, she seemed annoyed.

Walter was bothered by his friend's odd behavior, and he thought of asking for another transfer. But he stayed, and slowly began to see what the problem was. Louise had no outside interests. Her job was her whole life. As a result, she felt threatened when someone helped her with her work.

By learning about the whole person, Walter was able to understand Louise and to make allowances when she was irritable or silent. He knew that Louise's anger was not directed at him. And he was able to help her feel more secure by stressing her good personal qualities.

Walter learned another lesson that helped him to have good human relations. He learned that although people's reasons may not always be obvious, their actions usually stem from a desire to satisfy one of their needs.

Needs Affect Action

Sometimes when you try to fulfill your basic needs, you are aware of it. On a simple level, when you are thirsty, you take a drink of water. If you fear loneliness and have a need for companionship, you look up a friend. At other times, though, you may not be aware of what need you are trying to satisfy.

Knowing that people are trying to satisfy one need or another can help you to maintain good human relations. Like Bernice and Walter, you will not be quick to get angry with a person's behavior if you understand why the person is doing it. By understanding others, you can solve your own human relations problems. Here's an example:

Betty and Alyssa were salespeople in a large department store. When there was no work to do, they would chat for a while. Unfortunately, Alyssa often bragged: She did the best, she had the best, she was the best—on and on and on.

This can be annoying. But Betty was wise and had a sense of human relations. She guessed that Alyssa needed recognition. So Betty went out of her way to say something nice to Alyssa daily. Doing this, she helped to satisfy Alyssa's need for approval. As a result, Alyssa did not feel the need to brag so much, and Betty had solved her human relations problem.

It is not always easy to know what need motivates someone. Often it is impossible. Sometimes it is not necessary to know. However, knowing what motivates a person is a way to increase your understanding of his or her behavior.

It Takes Practice

It takes practice and patience to be able to display good human relations skills all the time. Sometimes you will have poor human relations skills. You will lose your temper. You will feel hurt or sad. You will decide someone is just not worth bothering with. But most of the time, it is not practical or useful to lose your temper.

These keys can help you understand others and build good human relations by making you consider what other people want and need and not just reacting to an immediate, surface situation.

Name _____   Date _____

Check Your Understanding

Understanding all you can about basic human behavior will help you to develop good human relations. You read about four keys for understanding people: (1) Everyone is unique. (2) Everybody wants to feel important. (3) People play many roles. (4) Your needs affect your actions.

Read the situations described below. Decide which key would be most helpful in understanding the person or situation and in developing good human relations. In some situations, you might decide that you would use more than one key. In the columns on the right, place a check mark to show which key or keys are most helpful in understanding the situation and in developing good human relations. After you have completed the exercise, compare your answers with those in the answer key on the last page of this chapter.

		1	2	3	4
a.	David was very absent-minded at work. Two minutes after he heard it, he could not remember what he had been asked to do. He was worried about making his next loan payment.				
b.	Linda and Juan worked together in the stockroom. They got along fairly well except for one thing: Linda had a small radio and played rock music all day. She liked rock music. She assumed everyone did. But it annoyed Juan.				
c.	Kimberly was a serious boss. Although she did not tell anyone, she worried about losing her job. She had a small child to support. She kept careful attendance records for the people under her supervision.				
d.	Cheryl became angry and upset when her boss publicly scolded her in front of other workers or customers.				
e.	Jason kept the windows open in the office, even on cold days. He liked lots of fresh air and thought everyone else did too.				
f.	Karen bored everyone she worked with by talking about how talented she was. She was always the first to seek praise and the last to give it.				
g.	Tim disliked Marie's habit of talking to herself while she worked. Although she usually finished her assignments before Tim, he complained to the supervisor and said she did not have her mind on the job.				
h.	There was something about his employer that Jack did not like. She never complained about his work, but she never said anything good about it either. Someday, he promised himself, he would quit.				
i.	Harold Torres was asked to recommend an employee to participate as a member of the employee-action committee. He decided to recommend Seth Nabors, a new employee. For a long time after that, Harold felt the coolness of two senior workers, Mary Riley and John Sandstrom.				
j.	No one liked being assigned to Sarah Snyder's work group. She wore you out with all her lengthy anecdotes.				

Case Study

In the situation described below, there is a human relations problem. Read the situation and then answer the questions to solve the problem. Write your answers in the space provided.

Katie prided herself on treating everyone the same and behaving the same way no matter where she was or with whom she was. When she began working on her first job as an assistant claims processor for a large insurance company, Katie kept her breezy manner in the office. She called everyone by his or her first name, or by a nickname if she thought of a cute one. Her pet name for Salvatore, an elderly policy holder, was Senile Sal. She did not mean any harm, she just thought it was funny.

Katie liked to use coarse language that shocked people. Her friends had always thought this was funny and "with it." She assumed that people in the office would think so too. Before Katie's probationary period was up, Mildred Foster, the manager, warned her about her behavior and language in the office. Ms. Foster also warned Katie about not showing respect for others.

"I really don't know what you're talking about, Millie," Katie said. "I treat everyone the same as I treat my best friends. What's wrong with that? And I don't talk any differently here than I do elsewhere."

Case Study Analysis

a. What is the real problem?_____

_____

_____

_____

b. What are the important facts to consider in this problem?_____

_____

_____

_____

_____

c. What solutions to this problem can you think of? Describe a few. _____

_____

_____

_____

_____

d. What would happen if the solutions you suggested were followed? Explain the results of each solution you described._____

_____

_____

_____

Name _____   Date _____

   e. Of the solutions you described, which would you recommend? Why? _____

_____

_____

_____

Personal Assessment

You all have undoubtedly had unpleasant experiences at one time or another. It may have been your fault, in that you made someone else feel like a nobody or overlooked differences that existed. Or it may have been someone else's fault, in that someone made you feel like a nobody or behaved in an unpleasant way.

On a separate sheet of paper, list some unpleasant moments you have had. Be prepared to describe these situations to the class. With your classmates, discuss which of the four keys to understanding others might have helped you deal with the situation.

Answers to Check Your Understanding: a. 3; b. 1; c. 3, 4; d. 2; e. 1, 4; f. 2; g. 1; h. 2; i. 2; j. 4.

Unit 1 Performance Mastery

Name _____   Date _____

A Working Vocabulary

Briefly define or identify each of the following terms. In the space provided, write your definitions or identifications using your own words. [Numbers refer to chapters where terms are introduced or discussed.]

Adult self (aspect) [2, 4, 6, 7,] _____

_____

Child self (aspect) [2, 4, 6, 7] _____

_____

Communication [unit opening] _____

_____

Environmental influences [3, 11] _____

_____

Genetic influences [3] _____

_____

Needs [2, 3, 4, 9, 11, 12] _____

_____

Parent self [2, 4, 6, 7, 12, 14, 16] _____

_____

Potential [2, 3, 4, 6, 9] _____

_____

Self-awareness [2] _____

_____

Self-conscious [1, 2] _____

_____

Self-esteem [2, 10, 11] _____

_____

Self-identity [2, 17] _____

_____

Values [1, 2, 3, 11, 12] _____

_____

Discussion

In the space provided, write your answers to these questions using your own words.

a. Why is good human relations important to you? _____

_____

_____

_____

b. Why must you understand people to have good human relations? _____

_____

_____

_____

c. How does knowing yourself help you have good human relations? _____

_____

_____

_____

d. What labels have been given to three aspects of our character? What do they signify?_____

_____

_____

_____

e. What five basic needs do all people have?_____

_____

_____

_____

_____

_____

f. What are the four different environments that help shape you? _____

_____

_____

_____

_____

g. What are the four keys you can use to help you understand other people and improve your relations with them? _____

_____

_____

_____

_____

Name _____ Date _____

Performance Assessment One

Your goal in this assessment is to recognize how important human relations can be to you by analyzing your everyday activities.

In the space given below, keep a diary of your activities for a full week—Monday to Sunday. Try to keep an accurate record of how you spend your time. Include conversations with classmates between periods as well as any other meetings you have with people as you go through the day. At the end of the week, analyze your activities by answering the questions that follow.

Monday _____
_____
_____
_____
_____

Tuesday _____
_____
_____
_____
_____

Wednesday _____
_____
_____
_____
_____

Thursday _____
_____
_____
_____
_____

Friday _____
_____
_____
_____
_____

Saturday _____

_____

_____

_____

Sunday_____

_____

_____

_____

a. How much time did you spend alone? _____
_____

b. How much time did you spend with others? _____

c. How much of what you did depended on others? _____

d. How often did you have to work at building good human relations? _____

e. What kinds of human relations problems came up?_____
_____

f. How did you handle these problems?_____
_____

g. How can you avoid these problems in the future?_____
_____
_____

Performance Assessment Two

Your goal in this assessment is to increase your awareness of how much people want to fulfill different needs and to recognize how this can influence their actions.

Collect advertisements from newspapers or magazines and list commercials on radio or television that are aimed at convincing people to buy the advertised product to satisfy some basic need. Determine which needs these examples focus on. Compare your examples in class.

UNIT 2

COMMUNICATION AND HUMAN RELATIONS

After completing this unit, you will be able to:

➤ *Identify connection between human relations and communication.*

➤ *Recognize two ways in which poor communication can hinder human relations.*

➤ *Identify abstractions that hinder communication.*

➤ *Avoid generalizations that hurt communication.*

➤ *Recognize four roadblocks to good communication.*

➤ *Recognize need to consider sources of information.*

You are always sending and receiving messages. Sometimes you do this consciously. That is, you are aware of sending or receiving messages. You know you are trying to communicate.

Often, though, you send and receive messages unconsciously. That is, you are not aware of what you are doing. You do not know that you are sending a message to those around you or that a message is coming in. Human relations is sending and receiving messages—consciously or unconsciously.

"Aha!" you say. "You're talking about communication." That's true, but in a very broad sense. Communication and human relations *are* almost the same thing—you can't have one without the other.

But have you ever heard the statement: "The whole is greater than the sum of its parts"? That statement is true in this

49

case. Human relations *is* communication, but it is also much more.

Certainly you cannot have human relations without some form of communication. And if human relations is to be helpful and productive for both parties, there must be good communication between the sender and the receiver.

It is possible that two people could be in a room together and make no effort to communicate. They could just be there and concentrate on whatever task they each have to do, ignoring each other. This would be an unusual situation. But even so, bad communication and human relations are taking place.

Any movement that one makes—or any noise, such as coughing or clearing one's throat—will give a message to the other person in the room. The message may have no real meaning as such, but the person receiving it may react. That person may express annoyance or leave the room suddenly.

In fact, that is what probably will happen if the two people in the room make no conscious effort to communicate and get to know one another. The absence of an effort to make contact sends a message, an unfriendly one. There is an old saying, "Silence cannot be misquoted, but it can be misinterpreted."

In other words, even when you are not consciously or deliberately communicating, you are sending a message. You are telling someone something.

It is human nature to reach out and communicate with others. If that effort is not made, you wonder why, or you take it as a sign of hostility or dislike. Thus, communication is basic to human relations.

In this unit, you will learn to develop effective communication and good human relations.

Chapter 5

GETTING YOUR POINT ACROSS

After completing this chapter, you will be able to:

> *Recognize two types of communication: verbal and nonverbal.*

> *Identify common communication problems.*

There are two forms of communication—verbal and nonverbal. Generally, verbal communication—writing or speaking—is conscious. Nonverbal communication also can be conscious. When you shake hands, pat someone on the back, or hit someone, you are communicating nonverbally, consciously.

Sometimes, you may frown without being aware of it, or smile without thinking. Then you are communicating unconsciously in a nonverbal way. How you hold your body communicates something. If your shoulders droop, your head hangs, and you shuffle along, you are telling people that you do not think much of yourself or that you are sad. At least, that is what most people would read into your body postures. You might not intend to send any message.

If you do not say "Good morning" or "Hi" or some such thing to your co-workers, you still are sending a message. In this case, your message is that you are unfriendly.

Knowingly or unknowingly, you are sending and receiving messages when other people are around. Those who know this probably will work to maintain a straight, alert posture most of the time so that a positive message goes out, even when they are not thinking about it. Such people will develop an attitude and appearance that sends a friendly, pleasant message, especially when no conscious effort is being made to communicate.

Nonverbal Communication

Nonverbal communication is the kind we use first, learning some of it almost automatically. Infants learn to smile as well as respond to threatening gestures or loving touches long before they can use verbal communication.

Society also teaches us a lot of nonverbal communication, such as looking people in the eye and shaking hands firmly. Nonverbal communication is used when people do not speak the same language. Highway traffic signs used throughout the world are nonverbal symbols. Types of nonverbal communication include:

- symbols

- body language

- proximity

- sign language

Symbols

Highway signs are a common example of symbols or pictures used to communicate. Humans have used symbols for nonverbal communication since ancient times. Before writing was developed, people would sketch a picture of an animal to convey meaning. Eventually, some pictures began to mean something else. For example, a picture of a lion could mean courage and one of a dove, peace, rather than the animals themselves.

Symbols can be a visible sign of something invisible. Examples of this are the notations made in music. Colors can be used as symbols. Red, for example, often symbolizes danger. Exactly what a symbol means is often determined by the culture.

Body Language

We are all familiar with body language and often use it consciously. It involves the use of hands, feet, posture, and facial expression. Much body language is learned behavior and influenced by the culture you grow up in. The most commonly used elements of body language are:

- eye contact
- hand gestures
- facial expressions
- posture
- tone of voice
- personal appearance

To some extent, your effectiveness at human relations relies more on how you speak rather than on what you say—more on your body language than on your message.

Most body language is an unconscious extension of your personality. But you can be aware of it and control it.

Proximity

Closely related to body language, proximity refers to the distance between people communicating. To understand this, visualize someone who is angry thrusting his or her face close to the other person. The angry person is being aggressive and it is not pleasant for the other person.

In normal communication, studies have shown, people have a personal space. If people other than close friends enter that space they feel uncomfortable.

The distance of this personal space is determined by a person's culture. In some northern European cultures, for example, the distance is about four feet. People feel comfortable communicating with people for business and other impersonal transactions at a distance of four to ten feet.

If you insist on getting closer than four feet with people not relatives or close friends, you may be damaging your public relations.

Sign Language

When you point or beckon, you are using sign language. A traffic officer uses sign language to control the flow of traffic. Sign language also means a specific series of hand motions and gestures conveying words and letters, which is used by deaf people.

Verbal Communication

Communicating through spoken words, or orally, is only one part of verbal communication. Verbal communication means *all* communication through words, including written words.

Good verbal communication—both *oral* and *written*—is essential to your success at school and at work, and in your relationships with others. If you can communicate clearly, and express yourself well, other people will understand you. Being able to express yourself on paper is also important. Can you clearly and concisely leave written instructions to a co-worker about how a job should be done?

Oral Communication

Oral communication—speaking and listening—is the more immediate form of verbal communication and most important in our human relations. Oral communication is a sensory-rich experience. You see and hear the person and can respond immediately. You see all the accompanying nonverbal communication as well.

Good oral communication skills are particularly important if your job like many jobs today involves telephone work. People get many of their communication cues from visual—nonverbal—signs. On the telephone, you cannot see the person you are talking to, and they cannot see you. You must get your point across clearly through your words, pauses, and tone of voice.

An often overlooked part of oral communication is one of its most important components—*listening*. If you do not listen to others, you are not communicating *with* them, you are only communicating *at* them. And that is not effective communication. When someone else is talking, or when you are reading written instructions, give the speaker all of your attention. Do not think about your response or jump ahead to other points. Concentrate on what the other person is trying to tell you.

Written Communication

Writing and reading are the other components of verbal communication. Written communication is not as immediate or as sensory-rich as oral. You are not face-to-face with the other person. You have time to think about what you write or read.

False Messages

When communication is unconscious, or unknowing, a person may send a false message, as Clyde did:

Clyde was an employee of a large airline company. His job was to check passengers in at the loading gate. He liked his work. He enjoyed meeting people and solving problems that came up. There was only one thing, although Clyde was not aware of it. He frowned a lot. He frowned when he was thinking. Sometimes he frowned because he was involved with a tough question.

The message that the passengers got was that Clyde did not like what he was doing, that he did not like them, and that he did not like to solve problems. "What a bad attitude," they thought. When the supervisor checked to see that the employees were doing their work properly, she thought the same thing. "What a bad attitude."

Fortunately for Clyde, the personnel department at his company was interested in solving problems, not firing employees. When they asked him why he did not like his work, Clyde was surprised. He said he did like it, and then they were surprised. "Well, you sure don't look it," they said.

With a little help, Clyde learned to relax the muscles in his face and to smile more on the job. At first, this was difficult. Clyde had to concentrate on it so that his nonverbal communication would not send a false message. But after a while, he smiled automatically—he stopped frowning—and he did not have to think about this particular nonverbal communication. He could let it happen unconsciously. Clyde stopped sending a false message.

Remember that you communicate in many different ways, consciously and unconsciously. When people are around, you always communicate—that is, relate—in one way or another. Sometimes when you communicate unknowingly, you send a false message. Keep that in mind when you receive messages too. The sender may not know that the message being sent is false.

Two-Message Problems

Here are two points you should be aware of when communicating so as to maintain good human relations:

1. More than one message may be sent at a time. These messages may contradict or support each other.

2. Sometimes, even when communication is conscious, a false message may be sent. (Or the receiver may interpret the message wrong.) In this case, the message is garbled, or confused, by either the sender or the receiver.

The sections below review these two communication problems.

Contradictory Message

Perhaps you have watched parents trying to reason with a small child who has just tried to cross a busy street alone because other children are on the other side. "You don't want to get hit by a car, do you?" the parents may say. "No-o-o," the child replies, all the time looking across the street and obviously wanting to go there,

cars or not. The child answers no, but nonverbal messages make it clear that a different message is being sent: "I want to cross the street alone."

The child is sending two messages at the same time. One is verbal ("No, I don't want to get hit by a car"). The other is nonverbal ("I want to cross the street alone"). One message says one thing, while the other says the opposite. It is like shaking your head when you say yes, and nodding your head when you say no.

Sometimes people are aware when they do this. Often they are not. People who like to be coaxed often will send two contradictory messages. "No, I don't want to play the guitar—I'm not very good, and no one wants to listen," a person may say. But the tone of voice carries an opposite message: "I'd love to play—please keep asking me."

People also send contradictory messages when telling you many times not to make a fuss about their birthday. If you do not, they are often hurt.

This kind of behavior is immature. It is important for good human relations to say exactly what you mean and to take others seriously when they say something. People will not enjoy being with you if they cannot be certain whether you mean one thing or exactly the opposite.

Garbled Messages

When you communicate and are not aware of it, you sometimes will send a false message, as Clyde did. But sometimes when you consciously try to communicate, you still may send a false message. Or—just as bad—the receiver may interpret the message wrong. How does this happen?

You are not likely to garble your message when communicating on a simple level. "How do I get to the post office?" "Go two blocks east on Main Street, turn left on Green Street. It's the first building on your right." The sender and receiver had no problems here.

However, people do not always communicate on this simple, concrete level. In fact, much of the time they communicate on a higher, more abstract level—that is, what they talk about does not really exist outside their minds. One cannot point to the postal system as one can to the post office building.

If one moves from talking about *where* the post office building is to *how* the postal system is run, the message becomes more abstract. The more abstract a message is, the more likely it is to be garbled by the sender or the receiver. That is, when one cannot refer to something physical (the post office building), the sender and receiver may have different abstract mental pictures (the postal system).

> "I don't think that the postal system is run well. There is too much waste."

> "What's the matter with you? You got something against postal workers?"

Something went wrong in that conversation. The first speaker could clarify the message by stating exactly what may be wrong with the postal system. Or the second speaker could ask, "Do you mean that postal workers are at fault?" Messages become garbled when people are not careful about the words they use and when they talk in general or abstract terms.

Two Word Problems

For effective communication and good human relations, it is worthwhile to consider words and how people use them. You will study abstractions and generalizations. An understanding of abstractions and generalizations can help you in your human relations.

Abstractions

In their haste to get a point across, people often tend to be sloppy speakers and thinkers. This results in ineffective communication and poor human relations. People often fool themselves by confusing words with things. This often happens with *abstractions*. As a simple example, take the word "dog." You may think this is a word that everyone can understand. Actually, "dog" is an abstraction. Two people may take it to mean two entirely different things.

Because of your experiences, for example, the word "dog" may make you think of a friendly, tail-wagging pet. But if you one day meet a mean, unfriendly dog and try to pet it, you may learn a painful, but useful, lesson: There is no such thing as "a dog" in the real world. "Dog" is a handy label for a certain kind of animal. But some dogs are small and hairless and others are large and shaggy. Some dogs are noisy and nervous and others are quiet and stately. Some dogs are timid. Others are aggressive. It is a mistake to think all such animals are the same. They are not.

Be careful not to confuse words with things. Avoid using abstract words as though they refer to only one thing that actually exists. A good way to guard against this is to try always to think of the specific object of the word that you are using—that is, the thing in the real world that the word refers to. The specific object is the thing you can see, touch, and describe in detail. If there is no single specific object for a word—it can mean many things—then it is an abstraction. Be careful with abstractions. They are necessary and useful, but they can be confusing.

As you have seen, "dog" is a useful abstraction. But it is only an abstraction. It does not have a single, specific referent. Every dog is different from every other dog. It can be confusing to ignore this fact. The words "my dog, Fritz," on the other hand, are specific. They refer to only one dog.

Generalizations

A *generalization* lumps together several words, things, or ideas and makes a statement about all of them without considering the individual characteristics of each. Generalizations usually begin with or include such words as "all" or "every."

Generalizations can be useful tools or language shortcuts. But like abstractions, generalizations can also result in confusion because they tell only part of the story but seem to be saying a lot. Consider the generalizations in this example:

"I'll *never* learn this job," Frank moaned. "*Everything* I do is wrong. *All* I *ever* do is make mistakes." In a moment of discouragement, Frank is making some wild generalizations about himself and his new job in a cosmetics plant. He has been working there for only two days—not enough time to make a statement like "I'll never learn this job."

During his first two days, Frank has done several things right. So it is untrue for him to say, "*Everything* I do is wrong. *All* I *ever* do is make mistakes." Frank is a better worker than he thinks. But his thinking is lazy and dangerous. If he continues to think this way, his generalizations will affect his attitude and his relations with others. He even may convince everyone that he cannot do his job.

Frank is generalizing in a negative way about himself. But it is also possible to generalize in a positive way. "This job is a snap. I know *everything* about it. I *never* make mistakes." Positive generalizations are as dangerous as negative ones. Both may lead to inappropriate behavior and poor human relations.

When you think about yourself or other people, abstractions and generalizations can be dangerous. You have to remember that they do not refer to something specific in the real world. Consider, for example, what might happen if you believed this generalization: "All bosses are bad and out to get me." At best, you would have an unhappy working life. Probably you would look for one job after another. No doubt some bosses are bad and do take advantage of workers. But a lot do not. Generalizations will not help you to communicate with and understand *your* job or *your* boss.

Avoid positive generalizations as well. They are no more helpful than are negative ones. "All jobs are great" is as silly as "All jobs are awful." Later on you will read about how to have good human relations by not generalizing about co-workers and the other people you meet.

Name _____   Date _____

Check Your Understanding

Communication and human relations are inseparable. Whenever people gather, some form of communication takes place. Sometimes, the communication is conscious. At other times, it is unconscious, or unknowing. But although communication is always going on, it is not always simple or clear. At times, you send false messages. You may send or receive two or more conflicting messages at one time. Communication, and thus human relations, may be clouded by abstractions and the misuse of generalizations. Read each statement below. Then select the phrase in the left column that best describes what is happening. Write the phrase number in the right column. You may use a phrase more than once. After you have completed the exercise, compare your answers with those in the answer key on the last page of this chapter.

1. communicating consciously

2. communicating unconsciously

3. sending more than one message

4. using abstraction

5. using generalization

6. sending false message

7. body language

8. good oral communication

a. "Well, you know what supervisors are. They are all a. ____ alike. If you've seen one, you've seen them all."

b. "Well, no, Ms. Crowley. I don't mind working a b. ____ little later tonight," Ramon said with a sigh.

c. Anna worked at the big bench, humming happily c. ____ to herself.

d. Lily enjoyed her job at the bank. The people were d. ____ friendly, and it was near home and where her friends worked. They would visit her at lunch. They all sat in front of the bank in Maria's flashy car.

e. "When you have finished polishing that fitting, e. ____ give it to Ricardo."

f. Claudio was eager to make money from the new f. ____ business deal. So when Isabel came into his office, he stood up, walked right toward her, and looked her in the eye to introduce himself.

g. Nicole called Pedro Torres and made her presenta- g. ____ tion. She smiled, paused before the end, and then tried to listen carefully to his reply.

h. You should go to the concert because all the h. ____ music will be great.

Case Study

In the situation below, there is a human relations problem. Read about it and then answer the questions to solve the problem. Write your answers in the space provided.

"I'm perfectly capable of picking it up myself!" Margot snapped as she knocked Ned's hand away. She snatched up the report she had dropped and slapped it down on her desk. Ned, his face burning, walked away.

"Hey, what was that all about?" LaDonna, who worked at the next drafting board, asked.

"Oh, men are all alike," Margot said as she began to work. "They think they are so superior."

"Gee, all he was doing was trying to help," LaDonna said.

"No. He was showing that men are strong and capable and that women are weak and careless," Margot said. "Just another male trick to keep us in our places."

Margot and LaDonna were drafting technicians in a large architectural firm. Ned was a senior architect.

"He's always pulling that chivalry stuff. Opening doors, getting up when I enter the room," Margot complained.

"He's been raised to act that way," LaDonna suggested. "Why don't you just explain to him that you would prefer for him to treat you as his equal?"

"Ha! He'd laugh in my face! He'd never accept me as his equal! All men think they're better than women!"

"A lot of them do," agreed LaDonna, "but not all of them. Take Ned, for example. He's a very sweet person, and he is always trying to help everybody. It would make no difference whether you were a man or a woman. He would still hold the door for you. That's just the way he is."

"Then how about Geoffrey?" Margot demanded. "Are you going to tell me he doesn't discriminate against women?"

"You're right," said LaDonna. "Geoffrey thinks women don't belong at the drafting boards. He says we are taking the jobs away from men. I've talked to him about it, and I think he's beginning to change his attitude."

"I don't believe it," said Margot. "He'll never change. None of them will. This company will always discriminate against women."

Case Study Analysis

a. What is the real problem?_____

_____

_____

b. What are the important facts to consider in this problem?_____

_____

_____

_____

Name _____   Date _____

c. What solutions to this problem can you think of? Describe a few. _____

_____

_____

_____

_____

d. What would happen if the solutions you suggested were followed? Explain
   the results of each solution you described. _____

_____

_____

_____

_____

e. Of the solutions you described, which would you recommend? Why? _____

_____

_____

_____

_____

Personal Assessment

Effective communication and good human relations go hand in hand. Think of some
times in your life when you experienced poor human relations because of ineffective
communication. On a separate sheet of paper, briefly describe these situations.
Identify what factors caused ineffective communication: false messages, conflicting
messages, careless abstractions and generalizations. Consider what you would have
done to change the situation and to improve your human relations. Have you
developed any communication flaws that damage your human relations? Be prepared
to discuss these situations and how they could have been avoided.

Answers to Check Your Understanding: a. Using generalizations; b. Sending more than one message;
c. Communicating unconsciously; d. Sending false messages; e. Communicating consciously; f. Body
language; g. Good oral communication; h. Using abstraction.

Chapter 6

DIFFERENT ROLE—DIFFERENT MESSAGE

After completing this chapter, you will be able to:

➤ *Identify the communication role played by the three aspects of character.*

➤ *Analyze which aspect of character controls your communication with others.*

To have good human relations, you must be able to communicate with all kinds of people. You must be able to communicate not only with members of your family and close friends, but also with co-workers, acquaintances, strangers, people your own age, people younger, people older, enemies and loved ones, people you work for, and people who work for you.

Communication may be classified into three general ways, depending on the receiver of the message.

One way is communicating with, for example, a younger sister or brother (*communicating down*). Communicating with peers—a friend of the same age—involves another (*communicating across*). Communicating with a supervisor, teacher, or older person (*communicating up*) is the third. Communicating up or down are *vertical communication*. Communicating across is *horizontal*.

Be careful when using these categories. They are based on generalizations. You do not always treat everybody in one category the same way. Your attitude depends on the situation. You talk differently with a stranger your own age than you do with a friend your own age. The categories are only guides to help you choose the most productive communication style for good human relations. Of course, you always base your communication on respect for the other person.

Being able to put people into one of these three groups will help you establish good communication. But remember that everyone is different. No two people are alike. For that matter, people do not always behave in the same way, react the same, or think the same way.

We All Play Many Roles

To maintain good human relations and have effective communication, you must be aware that every individual can and does play many roles during a lifetime—or even during a single day. These roles are determined by where you are, with whom you are relating, and what you are doing. For example, at home you may be a son or daughter, brother or sister. In school, a student, and in a part-time job a clerk, checker, or supervisor. In each role, you behave somewhat differently.

If you recognize the different roles you and others play, and if you deal with them effectively, you will have good human relations. Even though people behave differently at different times, good communication is always possible.

Three Aspects of Character

Whatever role people play, their behavior is also affected by the aspect of their character that is dominant. Recall the three basic aspects of character that all people share: the parent self, the adult self, and the child self. These terms, remember, are for convenience only. They do not mean a real parent, a real adult, or a real child. A real child has all three aspects of character, just as a real adult does. The parent self does not mean the role of parent.

Although everyone shares these aspects of character, they differ and are mixed differently in each person. Recall that the parent self is made up of the rules and teachings learned at an early age. When you use the parent self, you do not have to think much. You react with whatever built-in rule you have. The parent self wants to tell others what to do.

The child self is emotional. It is your creative, spontaneous side, and it wants others to make decisions. The child self wants to be told what to do.

Both the parent self and the child self tend to deal in abstractions and generalizations. Your parent self reacts on the basis of generalizations learned from real parents or from people who controlled you when you were young. The child self reacts with generalizations based on mental or emotional images, which are usually inaccurate.

Your adult self examines and questions each new situation before deciding upon the appropriate response. The appropriate response could be based on one aspect or on a mixture of two or three.

Which Character is Speaking?

To communicate best with others, you first have to know yourself. You can apply what you know about yourself to others. Then you will more easily see when someone is letting his or her child self take control, and you can respond appropriately. Or, you might tell yourself, "Oh, oh. I'm letting my parent self come on too strong in this situation."

Your Bossy Parent Self

When using your parent self, you tend to boss. You tell others what to do and what not to do. You often use words like *should* or *must*. Consider this example:

Cecilia had a strong parent self. In many ways, that was good. It made

her a good bank teller. She was punctual, accurate, careful, and dependable—all traits part of her parent self. She was such a good teller that the bank manager, Ms. Friend, promoted her to chief teller.

Now it might seem that having a strong parent self is the best thing for a boss to have. Not so. For Cecilia, it was the worst thing. She could not resist giving orders in direct, sharp terms.

"Benjamin, do it this way!"

"Rita, you must keep your cash record in this drawer."

"Matsuo, you should not talk to the customers so much."

Cecilia felt that everyone should do things her way. She had been a good teller. Now she was boss, and the other tellers must recognize this. It was for their own good.

Benjamin, Rita, and Matsuo did not recognize this. They did not think what Cecilia was doing was for their own good. They decided she wanted to be bossy and win approval from Ms. Friend. They began to dislike Cecilia. They worked less, and they gave her a hard time.

Ms. Friend saw what was going on. She talked to Cecilia about her human relations. Ms. Friend was able to show Cecilia that people do not like to be ordered around. They would rather be shown.

"Really," Cecilia said. "I thought that when I became a boss, I should just order people to do things."

"No," Ms. Friend said. "To get the most work, a boss asks people to do things. A boss rarely orders. Not good bosses, anyway."

Using Your Adult Self

Cecilia learned the lesson. She got her parent self under control and used her adult self more. If one of the tellers had played the child to Cecilia's parent self, communication between them might have been smoother, but it would not have been more productive.

Say, for example, that Benjamin's attitude at work was controlled by his child self. He would always want Cecilia to tell him what to do. He might even work below his potential on purpose so that Cecilia would order him around, correct him, and criticize him.

This would create a problem for Cecilia. She could be trapped into spending all her time making sure that Benjamin did the work right. She avoids this by controlling her parent self. She uses her adult self to deal with Benjamin. Rather than telling him how to do things, she encourages him to think and to use his adult self as well.

You should try to use your adult self in dealing with others. That will ensure effective communication and good human relations. Most other kinds of interaction are not productive, and they often result in anger or hostility.

Parent Selves Clash

If two people come on with their parent selves and both try to give orders, they will clash. This is true whether both are equals at work or one is in a superior position. If they trade opinions that both agree with, they will not clash. But if they trade opinions that both do not agree with, they will clash. Here is an example:

Calvin and Janet worked together in the shipping room of a large factory. They had to cooperate to make sure that the packages contained the right materials and were sent to the right places. They were good workers. But they both let themselves be controlled by strong parent selves. They each held opinions about everything. And their opinions did not often agree.

"You should type all the labels before putting them on the boxes," Calvin said.

"You should put the labels on as you type them," Janet said.

"You should fill the easy orders first," Calvin said.

"You should fill the hard orders first," Janet said.

"Television is great. I watch it all the time," Calvin said.

"Television is terrible. I never watch it," Janet said.

"Everyone should vote for Mr. X," Calvin said.

"Everyone should vote for Ms. Y," Janet said.

Calvin and Janet never took the time to examine what they were saying or hearing. They soon disliked each other a lot and could not work well together. As a result, customers' orders were not made up, or were sent to the wrong places or contained the wrong materials. Soon Janet and Calvin were both fired. If they had learned about themselves and had tried to control the parent aspects of their characters, they might still be working happily.

When the Boss is Bossy

Sometimes your boss or supervisor will play the parent strongly with you. That can be difficult and unpleasant. No one likes to be ordered about all the time or treated like a child. But if your boss behaves like that, what can you—one of the workers—do about it?

First, you can realize that the boss is acting out the parent self—giving orders, being strict, treating others like children. When your boss acts that way toward you, do not blame yourself or feel bad. You should not think you are always doing things wrong or behaving like a child. The boss's behavior is not under your control. You do not have to feel guilty or defensive when you have done

nothing wrong. Knowing what the real problem is will help you deal with it effectively.

The second thing you can do is react to the boss with your adult self. That is, show that you can do the work without constant direction. When needless commands are given, try to point out calmly that the work is being done and will be done when it should be. Usually people will respond to your adult self with their adult self. If the boss does not do so, at least she or he probably will be a less strong parent type over a period of time.

If you respond to the boss with your child self and show that you want and need constant direction and orders, you will strengthen the parent in your boss. And if you respond to the boss's parent self with your parent self, you probably will provoke a clash and solve nothing. The third thing you can do, then, is to avoid responding with your child or parent self.

Develop Your Adult Self

The most effective communication and the best human relations develop when people use their adult selves. You cannot expect everyone to do this, of course, but you can work to develop the adult aspect of your own character.

You can examine yourself and your values. A strong adult self has a system of values for making decisions and relating to people. You can learn the mechanics of making wise decisions. All these factors strengthen your adult self and thus build good human relations.

Here are some other things you can do:

- Learn to recognize the child aspect of your character. There are times when you will want to let the child self take over. It is the fun-loving, emotional side of you. It wants to be taken care of—everyone does, from time to time. It wants to be reassured. And it likes to daydream and fantasize. There is nothing wrong with any of this—in its place. At work, though, there are few occasions when the child self is appropriate. There is no place at work for temper tantrums, sulking, or avoiding responsibility. Learn to recognize your child self and control it.

- Learn to recognize the parent aspect of your character. Coming on strong with your parent self in any situation is not productive. And sometimes such behavior causes clashes. Probably your parent self has a lot of good, solid information and ideas to guide your behavior. But these ideas should be considered by your adult self before you use them.

- Learn to recognize when others are letting their child self or parent self control their actions. If the child self comes out, you know that the person needs reassurance, help, or just a kind word. If the parent aspect shows up, you usually can blunt or change it by reacting with your adult self.

- Silence is often an excellent tool for maintaining good human relations when you are communicating. Take a few seconds, whenever necessary, to sort things out before responding. Those few seconds of silence often can do more to build good human relations than anything you might say or do. "Count to ten before you act" is good advice. But while you count, think about the information you are receiving and consider what your response might be. Remember to let your adult self make this decision. Then act on it.

You Can Solve Communication Problems

Maintaining good human relations calls for your full attention. Even if you only communicate with close friends and relatives, you will have problems from time to time. But you must communicate with all kinds of people—those you know and those you do not know at all. At work, you must often cooperate with others and get them to cooperate with you. Depending on the situation, you and your co-workers will act differently at different times. Appreciate the differences and look for them. You now have some tools for dealing with your own behavior and that of others. If you want to, you can maintain good human relations with effective communication.

Name _____   Date _____

Check Your Understanding

Check to see whether you are on the road to having good human relations. The first step is to use the tools described in this chapter to identify your own behavior and that of others. Read each situation described below, in which two people are communicating—or trying to. Identify which aspect of character (parent, child, or adult) each person is using and decide whether they are having effective communication and good human relations. Write your answers in the space provided. After you have completed the exercise, compare your answers with those in the answer key on the last page of this chapter.

a. Diana was a night clerk in a pharmacy, where she worked with Ray, the night manager. Even though they knew each other well, Ray was impersonal toward Diana at work. He never called her by name. He was constantly telling her to do things, sometimes even shouting orders. Diana felt she was treated like a robot with no name and no feelings. She finally told him off and quit.

Character aspect Diana displayed: _____

Character aspect Ray displayed: _____

Communications were: (effective or ineffective) _____

b. On the last Friday of the month, work was piled up in the office where Felix worked. When he first arrived at work, Phyllis, his supervisor, told him that he should concentrate on finishing the monthly reports that day. Felix said, "Fine," and worked away on them. By lunchtime, he was half finished with the reports and was pleased because he thought he would complete them all that afternoon. Just before he left for lunch, though, Phyllis came up to him with some urgent typing to be done. "I've just got to have this typing completed," she told him. "Do it first thing this afternoon." Felix told her where he was on the reports and reminded her of her instructions that morning. After thinking it over for a few seconds, Phyllis said she would find some other way to get the typing done.

Character aspect Felix displayed: _____

Character aspect Phyllis displayed: _____

Communications were: (effective or ineffective) _____

c. When Ai Ching arrived at her office one morning, she found that her filing cabinet had been unlocked and left open. Nancy, who worked at the next desk, said she had opened the cabinet. "You had no right to go into my desk and take the key and open the file," Ai Ching said angrily. "How would you like it if I went through your desk?" "I was just trying to do you a favor," Nancy said, "and help you get started in the morning."

Character aspect Ai Ching displayed: _____

Character aspect Nancy displayed:_____
Communications were: (effective or ineffective)_____

d. It had been snowing all morning. Everyone in the department expected the office to close so people could go home. At noon, though, the word to shut down had still not been given. Everyone went to lunch. Later everyone returned to work except Ethel. The supervisor, Alice, checked to see whether anyone knew where Ethel was. No one did, and Ethel never called. At two o'clock, the office was closed because of the storm. The next day Alice called Ethel into her office and asked why she had not returned from lunch. "I decided to go home because the snow looked bad and I had nine miles to go," Ethel said.

"Other workers had to travel as far," Alice pointed out.

"I don't care," Ethel said.

"You know I can dock your pay for this," Alice said.

"My safety is more important," Ethel replied.

"Why didn't you at least call and let me know?"

"Oh, I just didn't think of that."

Character aspect Ethel displayed:_____
Character aspect Alice displayed: _____
Communications were: (effective or ineffective)_____

Case Study

In the situation below, there is a human relations problem. Read about it and then answer the questions to solve the problem. Write your answers in the space provided.

"Say, Ms. Wellman, do you know where the needle-nose pliers are?" Vince asked.

"They should be right there on the pegboard above the bench, Vince," Ms. Wellman said.

"Oh yeah, I see them," Vince said. He took them down and worked silently for a few minutes. Vince was learning to be an electrician by working in an appliance repair store. Ms. Wellman was the supervisor.

In the next few minutes, Vince asked Ms. Wellman several times where different tools were. Finally Ms. Wellman became annoyed and suggested that Vince look himself before asking.

Not much later Vince turned to Ms. Wellman again: "Do you think I should replace these parts, Ms. Wellman?"

"If they are worn, replace them," Ms. Wellman said.

"I'm not sure. Could you look at them?" Vince asked. Ms. Wellman did and told Vince to put in new parts.

Vince did, but in a few more moments he asked Ms. Wellman to show him how the new pieces should be attached. "Put them in the same way the old ones were," Ms. Wellman said.

Name _____   Date _____

"Well, I'm not sure I can," Vince said. "I'd like you to show me how it is done. I'd feel better." Ms. Wellman went to Vince's bench and put the new pieces in.

"Well, that job is done," Vince said shortly afterward. "What should I do now?" Ms. Wellman sighed and pointed to a pile of appliances waiting to be repaired. "Help yourself," she said.

"Well, I don't know which one to take, you know. Which one is more important? Maybe you had better tell me."

"They all have cards with the date they came in. Take the oldest first," Ms. Wellman said.

Vince went over and picked up one of the appliances. He took it to Ms. Wellman. "Do you think this is the oldest? Should I take this one?"

"Sure, sure," Ms. Wellman said, rolling her eyes. "That's fine."

Case Study Analysis

a. What is the real problem?_____
_____
_____

b. What are the important facts to consider in this problem?_____
_____
_____
_____

c. What solutions to this problem can you think of? Describe a few. _____
_____
_____
_____
_____

d. What would happen if the solutions you suggested were followed? Explain the results of each solution you described._____
_____
_____
_____
_____

e. Of the solutions you described, which would you recommend? Why? _____
_____
_____
_____
_____

Personal Assessment

During the course of your life, you will have to communicate with all kinds of people in many different situations. For one week, use the table given below to keep a record of all the different people you communicate with and then evaluate the record on the next page. Include those you just nod or wave to, as well as those you walk with or write to. You will talk with a few people more than once. Record the different character aspects you display in each encounter and use the initial for each aspect (parent, adult, child). Use arrows to show whether you communicated up, down, or across. If you cannot characterize an interaction, put a slash mark for each communication. Use this coding system:

Betty: P ↓, A ↓, C ↓,
Mother: C ↑, C ↑, A ↑,
Bill: A → A →, P →, C →
Mail Carrier: ///////
Teacher: C ↑, A ↑, C ↑, C ↑, A↑,

Monday	*Tuesday*	*Wednesday*	*Thursday*	*Friday*	*Saturday*	*Sunday*

Name _____   Date _____

In the space provided below, prepare, at the end of the week, a written summary of your interaction with five people with whom you communicated frequently. Include the following information about your communication patterns: (a) Did you mostly communicate with the child, parent, or adult aspect of your character? (b) Were you communicating up, down, or across? (c) Do you rate your communication as effective or ineffective?

1. _____
   _____
2. _____
   _____
3. _____
   _____
4. _____
   _____
5. _____
   _____

Answers to Check Your Understanding: a. Child, parent, ineffective;   b. Adult, adult, effective; C. Child, adult, ineffective; d. Child, parent, ineffective.

Chapter 7

COMMUNICATION ROADBLOCKS

After completing this chapter, you will be able to:

> ➤ *Identify four communication roadblocks.*

> ➤ *Recognize ways to overcome communication roadblocks.*

You have learned that communication can be hindered when people let their parent self or their child self control their relations with others. If you do not use your adult self to stop, think, and consider what is going on in a communication process, you often run into roadblocks.

What form can these roadblocks take? How can you recognize them and deal with them effectively? There are certain common roadblocks to good communication that you will meet often. In fact, the ancient Greeks knew about them. And way back in the Middle Ages, scholars gave them a name: logical fallacies.

Logical fallacy is just another way of saying communication roadblock—but it is more exact. It could be called a false argument, or faulty logic, or poor thinking. Whatever you call it, it results in poor human relations.

Some people use logical fallacies on purpose to make a point or to win an argument when they have no facts to support their statements. Other people use them without knowing it. Everyone is tempted to use them at one time or another. But logical fallacies mess up communication and weaken human relations. By learning about such communication roadblocks, you can recognize them when others use them and keep from using them yourself.

Verbal Personal Attacks

If you call someone insulting names, you will be communicating, but you certainly will not build good human relations. You will communicate dislike. Although that may be necessary sometimes, most of the time it is not. There are verbal personal attacks, however, that are not as obvious as an outright insult, but they also stop effective communication. Here's an example:

"Say, Frank," said Al, one of the workers in the S&W TV Repair Shop, "Carmen has figured out a pretty good way to check these old color sets. You ought to have her show you."

"Forget it!" Frank said. "Anyone who listens to the dumb music that Carmen does couldn't have any good ideas."

Did you notice what Frank did? He set up a roadblock to communication. Carmen's idea might not be good. But it might be excellent. Al thinks it is. Yet Frank ignores the idea. He does not even consider it. He just makes a personal attack on Carmen. He does not like the music she likes, and so he does not like any of her ideas. Since there is no connection between the type of music Carmen listens to and how she repairs television sets, Frank's reaction is foolish. Yet people do this sort of thing often. They ignore the topic or argument at hand and instead attack the person who puts it forward.

Sometimes people do this on purpose. Lawyers, for example, may use the personal attack as a tool of their trade. One lawyer put it this way: "When I have a strong legal case, I argue the law. When I have a lot of good facts, I argue the facts. When I have no case at all, I abuse my opponent."

Personal evaluations are sometimes important, of course. When deciding whether to vote for one candidate or another, you should consider facts about their personal characters. That is not a logical fallacy. Perhaps the health of the candidate is a factor: Is the candidate physically fit and well enough to serve? Some people said that President Franklin D. Roosevelt's policies were wrong because he was disabled. They were building roadblocks, just as Frank did.

There is a Latin name for this kind of logical fallacy that creates roadblocks to communication: *ad hominem*. It means "to the man" (or woman) and describes arguments that are aimed at a person instead of at an issue. You can dazzle your friends by calling their arguments *ad hominem* when they set up this kind of roadblock. The important thing, however, is to recognize it when others use it and to avoid using it yourself.

Counterattacking

The counterattack, "So are you," is another roadblock to communication. Everyone has used it. When you were a child, you used it almost automatically: "You're a liar!" "You are too!" You are most likely to set up this roadblock to effective communication when you are criticized or when your work is corrected. It is a way of defending yourself—you throw the criticism back at the other person. Here's how it works:

"Charles, I think you'd make fewer typing errors if you did not try to go so fast," Amanda said, trying to help her friend.

"I notice you never remember to cover your typewriter when you leave at night," Charles replied.

The conversation ends in a roadblock. Amanda may have had a good point. Charles would not know until he tried it. But Charles did not even want to listen to it. Instead, he found something about Amanda to criticize. Of course, she should cover her typewriter at night. But that has nothing to do with her suggestion about typing too fast.

Sometimes when someone says, "You're a liar!" it is logical to reply, "And you are too!" If both of you are already communicating on that level, what can you lose? But when you make an unrelated counterattack instead of responding to the issue, you are putting up a roadblock and damaging your human relations. Here's another example:

"Say, Marty. The inspectors said that the last few joints you welded were not as smooth as they should be. You know the company wants those welds nearly perfect."

"Oh yeah? Well I think the company should provide more parking spaces for the workers."

Marty jumped from welded joints to parking spaces without a second's thought. He tried to defend himself by attacking someone else. He would have been better off trying to find out how he could improve his work instead of playing "so are you."

Calling in the Experts

It is perfectly proper to quote experts to support a position you take or to turn to them for guidance. If, however, you do this in situations that do not warrant it, or if you do it in place of your own thinking, you are building roadblocks to communication and understanding.

Examples of this practice can be found by watching television. Thousands of commercials use this device to get people to buy their products. The message in the commercials is that because a certain well-known person uses the product, you should too. Such commercials are acting as a parent. If you believe them, you are letting your child aspect control you.

"Famous football players drive this car!" the commercial says, showing a famous player in one. The suggestion is that famous football players know a lot about automobiles, or that if you buy the particular automobile, you will become like the famous player. The truth is that most famous players do not know any more about cars than most other people do.

Cars, cosmetics, soap, and clothes are all sold by this technique. A famous person uses such and such a product—you should use it too.

"Doctors recommend . . ." or "Nine out of ten dentists say . . ."—these are appeals to authority to convince you to do something. Before being influenced by such appeals, consider them with your adult self.

If your doctor, after examining you, tells you to do something or to take a certain medicine for a specific reason, do it. But if an advertisement or a friend tells you to try Hogwash Mouthwash because doctors recommend it or because Stella Starlet uses it, forget it.

You will run into this communication roadblock many times. Friends, relatives, and co-workers will all use it now and then to convince you of something. You probably use it yourself. In Latin, this kind of fallacy is called *ad verecundiam*. It refers to an appeal "to revered authority." The fallacy comes in when the authority is respected for something that is not related to the subject at hand. (What do football players know about cars?)

Do not hesitate to raise questions when someone mentions an authority to back up a position. Examine the facts and decide whether the quoted authority knows anything about the field and is up-to-date. You can hinder your communication and human relations by blindly following authorities—especially when they are out-of-date. Janice learned that the hard way:

Janice was a darkroom technician at Modern Photos, Inc. She made excellent prints from the negatives she was given. Many people brought their negatives to the company because she did quality work. But there was one problem. Janice was slow. She was so slow, in fact, that the company did not realize a profit when she made the prints. And they could not keep up with the demand.

The company manager, Neal, tried to learn what the problem was. He wanted Janice to work faster without losing the quality of her work. He felt it could be done.

Neal quickly found out what the problem was. Janice insisted on washing all prints for 12 hours. She had been taught by an excellent photographer many years ago that it was very important to get all the chemicals off the picture.

"Look," Neal said to her. "With the new kinds of photographic paper we use today, you don't have to wash the prints that much. In fact, you only have to wash them for about four minutes. You can make your prints faster and still keep the same quality."

"Are you sure?" Janice asked. And she quoted what the famous photographer had told her: "If you do not wash them the proper length of time, they will turn dark."

Fortunately Janice decided to run a few tests, despite what her out-of-date authority had told her. She discovered that Neal was right and that she could shorten her work time.

Appealing to authority is fine. Make sure, though, that you also consider the facts of the situation at hand.

Overgeneralizing

"Just because I say I like sea bathing," Oliver Wendell Holmes, Sr., once said,

"that doesn't mean I want to be pickled in brine." He probably said that after having run into one of the most common and biggest communication roadblocks: overgeneralizing. You *overgeneralize* when you take one or two facts—or maybe just a part of a fact—and jump to conclusions. This habit weakens communication and human relations, and it can destroy your ability to listen.

Overgeneralization is probably the biggest roadblock to listening well. You listen to just a little of what someone is saying, and it sounds like something you have heard before. Thus, you immediately classify the speaker as "one of those." That person is a "liberal," or a "conservative," or a "union member," or whatever. You *know* what the speaker is going to say, so you stop listening. You have labeled the person in your mind on the basis of the generalization. In fact, the speaker may go on to say something quite different from what you expect, but you will not hear it. Here is an example:

Mindy began by saying, "Jules, when you type this report..." and that is all Jules heard. He knew Mindy. She was like all office managers. She was always giving needless directions. Jules had typed hundreds of these reports. He knew what to do. "Sure, fine. Yes, I understand," he said when Mindy finished talking.

He typed the report quickly and accurately, as he always did, and sent it to Mindy. Soon she was standing angrily beside his desk.

"Didn't you hear a word I said?" she demanded. "I told you this was a special report, to triple-space it, and also to put three-inch margins at the top and bottom. You typed it just like all the other reports."

Jules overgeneralized. It is all too easy to do that when one is in a familiar setting. Unfortunately, though, the habit makes people poor listeners, which—as in Jules' case—can result in doing the wrong thing at work. He *knew* all about typing reports. They were all double-spaced to him.

Resist the urge to jump to conclusions. Listen. Wait. Hear all the facts. Your generalizations may be appropriate most of the time. That is the problem. Most of the time is not all of the time.

Be on your guard against this type of communication roadblock when listening to people who are trying to convince you to do something. Such people often will take one small fact and blow it up into a very wide generalization:

- "If you do not vote for me, taxes will take half your income."

- "Students today don't care about their work."

- "Everyone on welfare is lazy."

- "There is so much crime and violence. People don't care about each other anymore."

When you hear people making general statements like those above, your mind should pick up a warning. Beware of the kind of thinking—or lack of thinking—that jumps from one small fact to a sweeping and unproved conclusion. At the same time, be careful not to read more than is intended into what someone is saying.

The fallacy of overgeneralization also has a Latin name: *secundum quid,* which means "according to something." Throw it into a conversation the next time someone sets up the overgeneralization roadblock. Do not fall into the *secundum quid* fallacy, or be taken in by it.

Avoid These Roadblocks

These are just a few of the roadblocks to effective communication and good human relations that you will meet. There are many others, but these are the most common. If you learn to recognize and avoid them, you will increase your potential worth and ability.

Name _____ Date _____

Check Your Understanding

Since good human relations depends upon effective communication, it is foolish to set up roadblocks and ruin your chances of making yourself understood. To see whether you understand the various communication roadblocks described in this chapter, read the situations given below. In the columns on the right, place a check mark to show which roadblock applies to each situation, using this list: (1) Personal attack (2) Counterattack (3) Calling in the experts (4) Overgeneralizing. After you have completed the exercise, compare your answers with those in the answer key on the last page of this chapter.

		1	2	3	4
a.	You turn on the television and Mika Morris, your favorite soap-opera star, is in a commercial for shampoo. "I'm Mika Morris, and being an actress, I need to wash my hair a lot. I use Radiant Hair Shampoo when I wash my hair; Radiant Hair—the best in America."				
b.	"Sandy, it looks as though you made an error on this column of figures. Can I help you find where it is?" "I noticed that you were late for work again this morning," Sandy replied.				
c.	"Once you've seen one slum, you've seen them all."				
d.	"Jeanne said that if we used oil on these fittings, we would get them undone a lot faster." "She's stuck up. I don't listen to anything she says."				

Case Study

In the situation described below, there is a problem. Read the situation and then answer the questions to solve the problem. Write your answers in the space provided.

Jim has been asked to serve on a three-member committee to plan the entertainment for the company's annual outing. The committee has decided to have a stand-up comedian and a country band with a singer. They have a long list of comedians and country singers, but they cannot decide which ones to ask.

"Look," Paul said, "Jo Reed is a very good singer. Let's get her."

"Did you see that article in the paper about her?" Jim asked. "I don't like her politics."

"What's that got to do with her singing, for goodness sake?" Marla, another member, wanted to know.

"I don't like the way she votes," Jim replied.

"Listen, she has been among the top country singers in the country for several years," Paul said. "I think it would be great if we could get her."

"You know who she supported in the last election?" Jim asked. "Maybe you don't care who you listen to, but I do."

"We're only hiring her to sing, not to make a speech," Marla said.

"Yeah, you just don't know what's going on in the world," Jim shot back.

Case Study Analysis

a. What is the real problem?_____

_____

_____

b. What are the important facts to consider in this problem?_____

_____

_____

_____

c. What solutions to this problem can you think of? Describe a few. _____

_____

_____

_____

_____

d. What would happen if the solutions you suggested were followed? Explain the results of each solution you described._____

_____

_____

_____

_____

e. Of the solutions you described, which would you recommend? Why?_____

_____

_____

_____

_____

Personal Assessment

Listen for the four common communication roadblocks in conversations that you have or that you overhear. You may hear them in the classroom, at work, at home, or out on the street. On a separate sheet of paper, make a record of the kinds of roadblocks you hear and bring examples of each to class. Be prepared to say how the communication could have been improved.

Answers to Check Your Understanding: a. 3; b. 2; c. 4; d. 1.

Chapter **8**

THE INFORMATION EXPLOSION

After completing this chapter, you will be able to:

➤ *Recognize that the information you receive includes both what is reliable and what is unreliable.*

➤ *Distinguish between reliable and unreliable sources of information.*

One of the biggest communication problems you face today is sorting out the huge amount of information that cries for your attention. Perhaps you have heard people say that we live in an *information age*. Television and radio stations broadcast information all day long. Personal computers connected to electronic bulletin boards or large databases make mountains of information available. Books, magazines, faxes, videocassettes, and newspapers pour out in a large, unending stream. Parents, teachers, friends, co-workers, and bosses all seek your attention and feed information to you.

Handling this steady flow of information is difficult. You shut a lot of it out in self-protection. But in protecting yourself, you must be sure not to shut out needed information. Before you act on or shut out information, it is important to consider where the information comes from—that is, its source. That will help you to decide how reliable it is and whether to shut it out.

At no time in your life will you receive more new information than when you are starting out on a new career. Then a confusing amount of information reaches you over a period of a few days or a few weeks. You must sort it out, accept some, reject some, act on some, and avoid acting on some. How do you do this? What guides are there for you to use?

Consider the Sources

At work, you may have three major sources of information: your supervisor(s), labor organizations—if they exist in your place of work—and co-workers. Most information will come to you orally—that is, it will be spoken. But on many jobs, it will be written as well.

Written information, of course, is usually more reliable and easier to handle than information received orally. You can study it at your own speed. You can think over what it tells you. You can refer back to it.

The sources of written information on the job usually will be your company or a labor organization. Written information can be passed on in several ways. It may appear as a notice on the bulletin board. Most companies have bulletin boards on which they post notices of interest to employees. And bulletin boards are also used by labor organizations to give information to union members.

As a rule, you can consider the information communicated on these bulletin boards to be reliable. In fact, you should check bulletin boards at work regularly. Many companies let employees use bulletin boards to communicate with one another. Notices of cars for sale or houses for rent can be found there. Usually, these notices are reliable also, but use more caution when acting on them. A person would be foolish to buy a used car without checking it first, even though a co-worker advertised it for sale on the company bulletin board.

Neither your company nor a union will back up messages other than their own on the bulletin board. Usually you can assume that notices posted by co-workers will be more reliable than those that strangers put in newspapers. Anyone who takes advantage of the bulletin board to sell worthless articles to co-workers will soon be very unpopular at work. But even though bulletin board messages at work may be more reliable than other types of messages outside of work, you still must be careful.

Other forms of written communication from the company could include a brochure that lists all the policies, rules, regulations, benefits, and history of the company. In addition, the company may include printed notices with your paycheck from time to time. You may receive a letter or a memorandum about something that affects only you. Many companies put out newsletters as well.

A labor organization will use similar written communication to give you information. Unions also often publish newsletters.

All this written information from your company and labor organization is useful and, for the most part, reliable. But remember that a company and a union will have different points of view.

Reliable Information

You may have heard someone say, "Put it in writing" when someone else made a wild promise. The purpose in saying this is usually to show disbelief. People are more willing to believe something that is put in writing than something that is only spoken, because the written statement can later serve as proof, or evidence. If everyone had to put everything in writing, people would be more careful about what they say. Although such a situation might strengthen communication, it also would slow things down. It is not practical to put everything in writing.

And so people talk a lot. In fact, you probably get much more information from talking than from writing. You will receive information from your boss and from a union orally. It is reliable too, but

not quite as reliable as the written word. With oral information, there is a greater danger that you will misunderstand or forget some part of it. And there is a greater danger that your company or union officials will not say exactly what they intend to say. Basically, though, you can rely on the information you receive from these people. Of course, you should examine it with the adult aspect of your character to see how their particular points of view may color it.

Misinformation

Misinformation is information that is wrong. Sometimes, people spread misinformation unintentionally. Perhaps they misunderstood something they were told, or read something that was itself incorrect. Unfortunately, some people pass misinformation deliberately. They may want to make themselves seem more knowledgeable or important, and so they go on and on about something they did or someone they know. Other people spread misinformation to cover up something they did wrong. In other words, these people lie.

Misinformation hurts. It hurts communication between people, because you cannot have effective communication if one person is lying. Misinformation may cost a company time and money as well.

For example, imagine that while transferring files from one directory to another on your computer at work, something went wrong. You gave the computer the wrong direction, and it erased your files instead of saving them. You know that those files are important, and you are afraid of what your supervisor will say. Instead of telling the truth, you tell your supervisor that the computer lost your files because of a malfunction. Your supervisor must call in a computer technician, and work in your department stops. Your inability to admit your mistake, and the misinformation you gave, will cost your department productive time and your company an unnecessary repair bill.

Make Up Your Own Mind

On the job, you will receive a lot of oral information from your co-workers. You must be careful when evaluating this information.

Long-time employees will usually try to be helpful, and for the most part they will be. However, they almost certainly will have feelings, complaints, or opinions that they have developed over the years. Without thinking about it too much, they will try to make their opinions yours.

Do not let them. Listen to everyone, but keep an open mind. Consider all the information you receive from all sources, and then make up your own mind about work conditions, other workers, the union, the boss, and everything else.

Long-time workers can give you hints about getting along on your new job. But be especially careful about acting on their advice when they talk about personalities.

Do not let them prejudice you against other workers, supervisors, or the company. Make up your own mind about people as you gain experience on the job. Marilyn and Arlene learned to do that.

When Marilyn went to work at the fish hatchery, Helen, an older employee, made an effort to welcome her. That was friendly of Helen. Unfortunately, though, one reason Helen did so was because she had no other friends among the workers. She had annoyed everyone else by her bragging and laziness.

Now she tried to prejudice Marilyn against all the other workers. Marilyn was bright enough not to let this happen. She was friendly to Helen. She thanked her for her help. But she also made a point of talking to and getting to know other employees. She made up her own mind about everyone.

When Arlene began working as a nursing assistant at Maryville Hospital, two or three older employees kept telling her how bad Donald, the supervisor, was. "You better watch him—he'll report you for anything," they said. "If you are one second late, you'll be in trouble. He's mean."

This information on the first few days on the job from "helpful," "friendly" co-workers began to make Arlene feel uneasy around Donald. That made it hard for her to learn her new job, which made her more uneasy. After about a week, during which Arlene did rather poorly, another nursing assistant, Theresa, talked to her.

"Donald asked me to talk to you," Theresa said. *"He thought you were getting too uptight and it would bother you more if he talked to you. Listen, Donald's a good supervisor. He's fair. I've seen a few people around here talking to you quite a bit. Don't let them scare you. You watch them a while and watch Donald. Then make up your own mind."*

Arlene did that. She began to see that the workers who complained about Donald and said he was tough were among the least productive workers. The ones who complained the most did the least work. They were often late and took extra time at breaks during the day. She saw that Donald had to keep after them all the time.

Arlene soon realized that if Donald was hard on the complainers, it was their own fault. She decided to make up her own mind about people in the future.

The Grapevine

The word for informal, oral communication among people is the *grapevine*. The use of *grapevine* to mean the informal spread of information began during the Civil War.

The expression "a dispatch by grapevine telegraph" was used to characterize unreliable information received by word of mouth rather than over the regular telegraph wires. The phrase became shortened to just *grapevine* applied to questionable information, which often turns out to be a rumor.

Today it is common for someone to say he or she "heard it through the grapevine." The grapevine is probably the source of most news and information you get in the world of work.

But you must be careful when handling information that comes to you by the grapevine. The information may seem clear, but often it has been distorted, blown up, or is completely wrong.

Rumors are one kind of message that spread through the grapevine. You know about rumors: They usually are untrue or exaggerated versions of a small truth.

It is not easy to ignore rumors because they often are about things that interest you.

You may want to believe them. You certainly want to listen to them. In fact, you enjoy them. You have to struggle to reject them or demand proof that they are true.

Another characteristic of rumors is that they are ambiguous—that is, they are not clear. They can be understood in different ways by different people. This ambiguity increases as a rumor is spread from person to person.

The children's game of telephone illustrates this. When the first person in a circle starts a word or short sentence by whispering it to the next person, it is usually quite different when it gets to the last person in the circle.

To establish good communication and human relations as you begin your career, keep yourself open to all sources of information.

Do not let one source crowd out the others. Listen to them all and weigh them.

Then form your own opinions upon which to base your actions.

Analyze Information

As you weigh information that comes to you, always consider the source. Whether the source is a company official, a union official, or a co-worker, you can assume that the information will reflect the interests and point of view of the source. There is nothing wrong with that as long as you recognize it. When you pass on information, you cannot avoid coloring it according to how you see it. Because of this some information will reflect reality more carefully and accurately than other information will.

Written information is more easily dealt with and, generally, more reliable than oral information. Most information you receive on a day-to-day basis at work will be oral.

Most rumors are not passed along in written form. Be slow to accept unwritten information. Always try to verify it either by actual observations of your own or by seeking further information from other sources.

Name _____   Date _____

Check Your Understanding

Before acting on information, you should know how reliable it is. To know that, you must consider its source. Read the situations described. In the space provided, say whether the source is the company, the union, or co-workers. Rumors could come from all three sources. Evaluate how reliable the information is likely to be. After you have completed the exercise, compare your answers with those in the answer key on the last page of this chapter.

a. "You don't have to work that hard. Are you trying to make the rest of us look bad?"

    Source: _____   Evaluation: _____

b. A bulletin board notice said that the new work hours were 8:30 a.m. to 4 p.m.

    Source: _____   Evaluation: _____

c. Julie, the plant manager's secretary, told you that she heard the company was going to change to a four-day workweek.

    Source: _____   Evaluation: _____

d. A union notice on the bulletin board said there would be a meeting today at 4:30 p.m.

    Source: _____   Evaluation: _____

e. Philip, a union steward, said that he heard the company was going to lay off ten percent of the work force.

    Source: _____   Evaluation: _____

Case Study

In the situation below, there is a human relations problem. Read about it and then answer the questions to solve the problem. Write your answers in the space provided.

Otis got home from work about 20 minutes before his wife did, but he was too upset to do anything about starting dinner, or even to sit down and read the paper. The minute Naomi walked in the door he started telling her what happened.

"You won't believe what I found out today!" he exclaimed. "They're going to put us on rotating shifts! That means I'll never get used to one schedule, and I'll be tired all the time. I hate it! I'll quit and apply for a job at United Machine in Pleasantville."

"Wait a minute!" said Naomi. "Who told you all this? Jorgenson, the supervisor?"

"No," said Otis. "Jenny Piacenti, who works at the next bench."

"But how did she know? Was there a notice on the bulletin board?"

"I don't know. I don't look at the bulletin board—it's got too much stuff on it that doesn't interest me. Harry Nakamura told Jenny, and he's a pretty smart guy."

"Maybe he's smart," said Naomi, "but that doesn't say where he got his information. Did you ask your union shop steward about it?"

"No, I never thought of that. Maybe I should. But I wanted to get right home to tell you. I want to go over to Pleasantville as soon as I can to look for another job."

"But, Otis," Naomi said. "Pleasantville's a long drive. Don't you think you should find out whether this change is really going to happen before you do anything? Don't you have anything in your contract about rotating shifts? We do at the electronics plant."

"Naomi, have you really read your union contract? I didn't think anyone but the officers did that. Besides, Jenny said she was sure that it was true."

Case Study Analysis

a. What is the real problem?_____
_____
_____

b. What are the important facts to consider in this problem?_____
_____
_____

c. What solutions to this problem can you think of? Describe a few. _____
_____
_____
_____

d. What would happen if the solutions you suggested were followed? Explain the results of each solution you described._____
_____
_____
_____

e. Of the solutions you described, which would you recommend? Why? _____
_____
_____
_____

Personal Assessment

Written information is usually more reliable than oral information. However, even written information can be slanted to reflect a point of view. Careful readers consider this when evaluating and acting on written information. Obtain at least three copies of newsletters, or brochures put out by local companies and by unions. Study the contents. Look for stories about the same or similar topics in different publications. Try to see how each source interprets and slants the information. On a separate sheet of paper, list the sources and outline their points of view. Be prepared to say which source is most reliable and why.

Answers to Check Your Understanding: a. Co-worker, unreliable; b. Company, reliable; c. Co-worker, unreliable; d. Union, reliable; e. Co-worker, unreliable.

Unit 2 Performance Mastery

Name _____ Date _____

A Working Vocabulary

Briefly define or identify each of the following terms. In the space provided, write your definitions or identifications using your own words. [Numbers refer to chapters where terms are introduced or discussed.]

Abstraction [5, 6] _____

_____

Calling in the experts (*ad verecundiam*) [7, 12] _____

_____

Communicating across (horizontally) [6] _____

_____

Communicating down/up (vertically) [6] _____

_____

Grapevine [8] _____

_____

Generalization [5, 6, 7, 11, 12, 15, 16] _____

_____

Good listening [7] _____

_____

Logical fallacy [7] _____

_____

Misinformation [8] _____

_____

Personal attack (*ad hominem*) [7, 12] _____

_____

Rumor [8] _____

_____

Discussion

In the space provided, write your answers to these questions using your own words.

a. What two common problems are you likely to meet when you communicate?

_____

_____

b. Why must you be careful when dealing with abstract terms and emotions?

_____

_____

_____

c. What can happen if two people let their parent aspect dominate when they communicate with each other?_____

_____

_____

_____

d. What are some things you can do if your supervisor always displays the parent aspect of his or her character? _____

_____

_____

_____

e. What are four common roadblocks to effective communication? _____

_____

_____

_____

f. How can overgeneralizing weaken good communication? _____

_____

_____

_____

g. Why is it important to consider the source of the information you receive? __

_____

_____

h. What are three major sources of information at work? _____

_____

_____

i. How does the grapevine work and how reliable is it as a source of information?

_____

_____

_____

Name _____   Date _____

   j. What is misinformation and how is it harmful? _____

_____

_____

_____

   k. What are four examples of nonverbal communication?_____

_____

_____

_____

Performance Assessment One

Your goal in this assessment is to demonstrate your awareness of the need to communicate with different people in different situations.

Role-play with members of your class in the situations described below. Two members of the class will take part in each of the situations. They decide which aspect of their character (parent, child, or adult) to display. In the space provided, evaluate the exchanges and try to identify the character aspects displayed, roadblocks set up, and other communication problems. The situations are:

   a. A police officer with a motorist stopped for speeding.

   b. A supervisor warning a worker about being late.

   c. A teacher with a student who has failed to complete an assignment.

   d. Two good friends who are supporting different candidates for public office.

   e. A salesperson working with a customer who is returning some faulty merchandise to the store.

   f. A union official and a company official meeting to discuss a higher wage scale proposed by the union.

_____

_____

_____

_____

_____

_____

_____

_____

_____

_____

_____

_____

_____

_____

_____

_____

_____

_____

_____

_____

_____

_____

_____

_____

_____

_____

_____

_____

_____

_____

_____

_____

_____

_____

_____

_____

Performance Assessment Two

Your goal in this assessment is to recognize how often communication roadblocks occur and to identify them.

For a period of two weeks, collect written samples of communication roadblocks that you read about in Chapter 7. Identify the roadblock in each sample and tell how it can be avoided. Look for examples in magazines and newspapers, especially in letters to the editor, editorial pages, articles by columnists, and stories quoting politicians. At the end of two weeks, compare and discuss your examples with those of your classmates.

UNIT 3

HUMAN RELATIONS AND YOUR CAREER

After completing this unit, you will be able to:

➤ *Match your own interests and skills with career requirements.*

➤ *Demonstrate how needs, motivation, and the will to work are related.*

➤ *Identify factors that influence morale and job satisfaction.*

➤ *Recognize the differences between positive and negative attitudes.*

➤ *Identify several characteristics of effective leadership.*

You are aware that you have to develop good human relations skills to succeed in any career. You also know that relating to other people is not simple: Every individual is a complex mixture of different value systems, different outlooks, and different reactions.

Although there are no quick, easy rules that ensure that you will always have ideal human relations (you will not), you have learned some basic concepts that can help guide your behavior and reaction to others. These concepts, discussed in Unit 1, are: everyone is unique, everyone likes to feel important, you must consider the whole person, and needs affect actions. The basic needs that all people share are the need to keep alive (food, drink, shelter), the need to be free of fear and anxiety, the need to be loved, the need to be admired and respected, and the need to realize your potential.

95

These concepts can help you to understand yourself and others and to anticipate problems so that you can avoid them. Your *motivation* stems from your desire to satisfy your basic needs. How you view these needs will determine how highly you are motivated. For most people, the physical needs of keeping alive and being safe are satisfied fairly easily. The needs for love, respect, and realizing your potential are met less easily. As a result, much of people's motivation stems from their efforts to fulfill these needs.

Some people are highly motivated. Their need for love, respect, or self-realization is strong. They may try to meet many of these needs outside of work. But careers make up such an important part of most people's lives that they generally will try to satisfy these needs through their work.

Sometimes people's strong needs cause them to set high career goals. When they do not achieve these goals, they become frustrated and tense. They cannot relate well to others. Such a situation may cause them to work even harder. Or they may stop and take time to rethink things. They may decide that their goal is beyond their abilities. If so, they try to set other goals. They are happiest, and they have the best human relations, when their goals and their achievements match. In this unit, you will learn what is involved in satisfying the greatest number of needs in a successful career. A first step is finding the right career.

Chapter 9

THE RIGHT CAREER FOR YOU

After completing this chapter, you will be able to:

➤ *Recognize the six main categories of working requirements.*

➤ *Identify your talents, skills, interests, and hobbies and compare them to the requirements for careers that interest you.*

Working is a necessary fact of life. Through work, you support yourself and your family, you contribute to society, and you meet your personal goals. Working can be a fulfilling and rewarding experience, or it can be drudgery.

The Perfect Job

What is the perfect job? It is a job where your needs are met, your goals realized, your values and personality taken into account, and your talents and skills used and expanded. In other words, there are as many possible "perfect" jobs as there are workers in the workplace. Everyone would define her or his perfect, or ideal, job differently. It is important, when you start thinking about your future, to define what it is you want from work. Sometimes, families expect that you will follow in your parent's footsteps. You may want to do that—but sometimes, your parent's career may not be the best one for you. That was the problem facing Jared in this example:

Jared's father and mother were lawyers. His grandfathers were both lawyers. Even one of his great-grandfathers was a lawyer! Jared grew up in a house where a lot of attention was focussed on a legal career. From the time he was young, Jared's parents assumed that some day he would join them in their law firm, the firm that his great-grandfather had founded.

Jared assumed that also. He was intrigued by what his parents did. Like them, he considered law a challenging and interesting profes-

sion. But, sometimes, Jared got a little scared about seeing his future all mapped out for him. Sometimes, he wondered if he wanted to spend all his time inside, wearing a suit, preparing legal briefs and arguing cases.

Jared did fine in school; he was a good student, but not a great one. When he was a sophomore in high school, he took the required shop course. To his surprise, Jared loved it—he really enjoyed working with his hands. He especially loved auto mechanics.

When he turned 16, Jared bought an old car and spent hours fixing it up. He started helping his friends tune up and repair their cars. He even fixed his parents' cars a few times.

As the year went on, Jared's parents began talking about college. When they attended the school college fair, Jared picked up brochures from the near by technical college. It offered academic courses as well as courses in auto mechanics. Jared realized that he did not want to be a lawyer—he wanted to spend his time fixing cars. He wanted to figure out what was wrong and solve the problems. Now he had to tell his parents that this was what he wanted to do.

It may not be possible to find a job that matches you and your requirements perfectly. However, through self-knowledge, and through knowledge of the workplace, you can focus your attention on careers that interest you. For example, if you have poor drawing skills, you would probably not pursue a career in fine arts or drafting. If you enjoy people and like being helpful, a job that required you to be alone many hours a day would not be ideal. If you are a "night owl", a job working second or third shift might suit you best.

Different Jobs Need Different Workers

Each job and each career path has a set of unique requirements. The U.S. Department of Labor has defined six main categories of working requirements to consider:

1. Training
2. Aptitudes
3. Interests
4. Temperament
5. Physical Requirements
6. Working Conditions

By measuring yourself against the requirements for a particular job, you can test to see if a job is suited for you.

Training

Different jobs require different levels of education and training. Even within the same type of job—such as engineering—there are different areas of specialty. You could be a mechanical engineer, an electrical engineer, an environmental engineer, a nuclear engineer, a civil engineer, or an industrial engineer. Although each type of engineering requires the same broad background in mathematics and

science, each also requires further specialized training. If you dislike science and math, chances are you would not even consider a career in engineering.

Almost all jobs require a high school diploma, or the equivalent. Many secretarial and bookkeeping positions can be filled by students right out of high school. Some jobs require at least four years of college—for example, teaching or accounting. Others, such as hairdressing, lab technician, practical nursing, or computer programming, require a year or two at a special school.

In addition, many jobs require a period of training. Each workplace operates differently, and therefore needs to train workers in the unique requirements of that workplace. This training period can be short—a few hours of orientation—or long—two to three years of apprenticeship.

You should look into the training requirements for a job or career that you want to pursue. Then ask yourself:

• Is it achievable?

• Will I commit myself to the months or years of schooling that are required?

Aptitude

Your natural talents and abilities determine your aptitude for a particular job. Aptitude is as important as training. All the education in the world will not make a fine athlete out of someone with poor hand-eye coordination. When you combine training and aptitude, however, you have the basis for a successful career.

Each occupation requires different abilities, but most jobs share some aptitude requirements. To be successful, you need an aptitude for learning. You must be able to learn and understand new information. You need good verbal ability to communicate well with others. An aptitude for numbers is helpful in all careers. Good motor coordination is also important. In some jobs, such as dental hygienist, designer, and some factory jobs, manual dexterity is important.

Interests

If you have the aptitude for secretarial work, but no interest in it, you are not likely to pursue it as a career. A rewarding career is one that interests you. You will overcome obstacles to train yourself and find work in a field in which you are interested. Interest is a broad requirement. If you like the outdoors, and are interested in nature, you might find yourself drawn to careers as diverse as forest ranger, marine biologist, or gardener. Chances are, you will not be interested in a job that requires you to be inside all day, such as a stockbroker. If you like to work with others, you might want to be a salesperson, a receptionist, a teacher, a psychologist, or a politician. You would be less likely to enjoy a job where you are isolated from others, or where interaction is limited, such as on a noisy assembly line.

Temperament

Some people are extroverts—friendly, gregarious, needing others around. Others are introverts—quiet, reclusive, or shy. Can you imagine an introverted car salesman? He would not be temperamentally suited to the job.

Some people like to be in charge—they find it hard to keep silent if they see something being done incorrectly or inefficiently. Their temperaments suit them for jobs that give them a great deal of autonomy, or independence. Or, if they are organized, they may have the ideal temperament for being a group leader or handling an event that requires planning and coordination. They would be unhappy, and probably perform poorly, in a job that was narrowly defined and offered no ways to correct inefficiencies.

Physical Requirements

Every job has a physical requirement. You may think immediately of a physical job being one that requires standing, lifting or walking—cashiers, longshoremen, or mail carriers all have jobs with different, often strenuous, physical requirements. But even sedentary jobs, such as writing, secretarial work, and computer programming, have unique physical requirements. These sit-down jobs often strain back, neck, and arm muscles because of the repetitive nature of the actions performed.

Compared with the past, employers today generally are more aware of the toll that the physical stress jobs take on a worker. They have expert studies that point out physically stressful actions and alternatives.

The addition of women and disabled workers to the workplace has also changed the definition of some jobs that were traditionally considered occupations for able-bodied males only. Women work side-by-side with men in jobs from engineering to construction.

People who formerly were considered unemployable because of physical or mental handicaps are making important contributions to the workplace.

Working Conditions

The working conditions required in a particular job or by a certain career path are important considerations as you search for the right career for you. There are two main types of working conditions: physical conditions and psychological conditions.

Physical Conditions

The physical conditions of a job include such things as whether the job is indoors or outdoors; whether you will work in a noisy or quiet environment; whether you will be exposed to extremes of temperature; whether you might die just by doing your job (police officers and fire fighters); and whether dangerous or unhealthy atmospheric conditions lead to occupational diseases, such as black lung disease, asbestosis, or industrial asthma.

The physical stresses of certain jobs are so great that only people with strong motivation will apply. Legislation enacted by state and federal governments helps to protect workers from some of these physical hazards, but it is impossible to make every job 100 percent safe.

Psychological Conditions

Physical conditions refer to tangible job conditions. Psychological conditions refer to intangible conditions of a job—the work climate or style of a company rather than the physical climate.

Is the job relaxed? Are the people easygoing, or is the climate of the workplace fast and tense? Are people regimented, or are they allowed to do what they want, when they want, as long as the work gets done?

The work climate is influenced by the size of the company as well as the type of work done. It would be impossible to be a relaxed and laid back commodities broker on the floor of the New York Stock Exchange. In the example below, Grace-Anne had problems adjusting to a new job because the work climate did not suit her temperament.

Grace-Anne had been working as a free-lance graphic artist when she decided to apply for a job in the advertising layout department of her local newspaper. Although Grace-Anne really enjoyed her work, she was beginning to feel a need for more security than free lancing could offer.

Her interview went well, and Grace-Anne was hired. At first, she enjoyed the challenges of her job. It was exciting having a specific place to go each day, and knowing that she would receive a consistent paycheck at the end of each week. Soon, however, the novelty of her new job wore off, and Grace-Anne started to dread the daily grind.

The newspaper was a fast-paced place to work. There was little or no time for the kind of creative work Grace-Anne enjoyed most. She missed the freedom of making her own hours. She was not able to turn down jobs she did not want to do, as she could when she was her own boss. She resented people changing her designs or stealing her ideas.

Grace-Anne had not worked at the newspaper long before she realized that the work climate did not suit her. She decided that the freedom of being her own boss was more important than the security of a paycheck each week.

How Do You Choose the Right Career?

It may seem overwhelming, as you survey the many choices confronting you in the job market, to decide what you want to do with your life. Some people seem to know in what direction their life is headed from the time they are very young. Others may experiment, moving from career to career and job to job, acquiring skills and knowledge and learning more about different job requirements.

Still others may be paralyzed by fear of the unknown, staying with a job they are not well-suited for out of fear of change or failure.

How can you know which career is right for you? Educating yourself about different careers and their requirements is probably the best way. Working part-time and during school vacations, you can experiment with jobs and see which types of work you are most suited for.

Critically evaluating your personality traits, needs, and values is another way of focusing your search and discovering what you want out of life.

Examining your hobbies and activities will help you identify traits that could lead you to certain careers.

Name _____   Date _____

Check Your Understanding

There is no perfect job. The job that will be ideal for one person will not be good for someone else. Read the personality profiles in column A and the job descriptions in column B. From the information given, choose the worker who most successfully matches the job requirements. After you have completed the exercise, compare your answers with those in the answer key on the last page of this chapter.

A	B	
a. **Yinong**—enjoys detail work, has good math skills, prefers working alone	**Auto Repair Stockperson**—fill mechanics' orders, keep track of inventory, some heavy lifting	
b. **Latoya**—Student Council president, organized, energetic, enthusiastic, good writing ability	**Cashier**—for busy department store; may involve filling in at Courtesy Desk on occasion	
c. **Jake**—likes to fix motors, athletic, quiet	**Bookkeeper**—small cleaning service; flexible hours	
d. **Isaac**—argumentative, loud, opinionated, athletic, likes to work on cars	**Public Relations Apprentice**—organize and publicize community events for local hospital	
e. **Mary-Kate**—inquisitive, enjoys research, good verbal ability, outgoing	**Parks and Recreation Employee**—responsible individual to work alone, maintaining city park and doing minor repairs on equipment	
f. **Dwayne**—good math skills, organized, efficient, friendly, eager to please	**Newsroom Intern**—for weekly paper; main responsibility to report on community activities	

Case Study

In the situation below, there is a human relations problem. Read about it and then answer the questions to solve the problem. Write your answers in the space provided.

Rosanna was an excellent student. She liked school—the atmosphere, the excitement, learning new things. She even enjoyed doing homework. Rosanna knew that she wanted to be a teacher when she graduated. Rosanna joined the Future Teachers Club. Her favorite part of the club meetings was when the students discussed new trends in education or new ways to teach old subjects. She enjoyed planning parties and activities for children, but felt a little removed from the children when the party was taking place. Rosanna thought maybe she just was not suited to teaching young children, and by senior year had decided to major in secondary education at college.

Rosanna had no trouble excelling in her college courses. She had innovative ideas that earned her high marks and approval from her professors. There was only one problem—Rosanna did not enjoy teaching. She was lost. All her life, she had planned to be a teacher. As graduation day approached, Rosanna felt increasingly depressed. What would she do with her life?

Case Study Analysis

a. What is the real problem?_____

_____

b. What are the important facts to consider in this problem?_____

_____

_____

_____

c. What solutions to this problem can you think of? Describe a few. _____

_____

_____

_____

d. What would happen if the solutions you suggested were followed? Explain
   the results of each solution you described._____

_____

_____

_____

e. Of the solutions you described, which would you recommend? Why? _____

_____

_____

_____

Personal Assessment

Deciding on a career may seem overwhelming. However, you already have clues to
what jobs you are suited for. These clues are present in your choice of hobbies, course
of study, part-time jobs, social activities, and friends. By looking closely at what you
know about yourself, and by comparing that with the requirements for different jobs,
you have begun.

Use a separate sheet of paper. Divide it into seven columns. This will be your
Personal Inventory Sheet. Write the following words at the top of each column: My
Talents and Abilities, Things I like To Do, Things I Dislike Doing, My Favorite
Subjects, My Least Favorite Subjects, My Hobbies, Jobs I Have Enjoyed (include
volunteer jobs and school committees, etc.). Be honest with your answers.

On another sheet of paper, create a Job Requirements Sheet. List three jobs that
interest you. Under each job, write down the requirements of the job: Training,
Aptitudes, Interests, Temperament, Physical Requirements, and Working Conditions. Do some research; talk to someone in those fields. Evaluate your findings. How
does your Personal Inventory Sheet match with your Job Requirement Sheet?

Answers to Check Your Understanding: Auto repair stockperson—Isaac; Cashier—Dwayne; Book-
keeper—Yinong; Public Relations Apprentice—Latoya; Parks and Recreation Employee—Jake;
Newsroom Intern—Mary-Kate.

Chapter 10

YOUR ATTITUDE COUNTS

After completing this chapter, you will be able to:

> ➤ *Identify positive and negative attitudes.*

> ➤ *Evaluate the attitude of others around you.*

> ➤ *Recognize that attitude affects human relations.*

Dulcie thought of herself as clever. She also saw herself as an individual. She did her own thing. Work was a necessary evil to her. If she did not make it at one job, she would at another, she thought. So why worry? She did not think in terms of a lifelong, satisfying career. She thought in terms of a day-to-day existence, working only as necessary.

Dulcie's first job was in a bank. She wore her jeans and T-shirts to work. They were "her personal style." She sometimes wore her bathing suit under a tank top with shorts. She considered herself a night person—which made getting up in the morning hard. She was often late.

Dulcie did not let her job interfere with the important activities in her life. If there was a rock concert, or a party, she would call in sick and take the time off. The next day, she would brag to her co-workers about the great time she had had.

At the end of her trial period, Dulcie was out of a job. At first, she enjoyed the freedom of being unemployed. But after a few weeks, she began to wonder why she was having trouble finding another job. Something seemed wrong.

What was wrong with Dulcie? A lot of things. But they can all be summed up in one word: attitude.

Attitudes Affect Behavior

Attitude is your state of mind. It is your feelings about your life. Your attitude is reflected in your behavior. It affects how you carry yourself, how you talk, and how you do your work. Your attitude reflects all the other things you have been reading about: motivation, morale, values, and goals.

Your attitude shows how you put all these things together and present them to the world. It is what is out front. And the world will judge you pretty much on the attitude you present. Bruce found that out:

Bruce could be a good electrician. He had done well studying it in school. He looked forward to the day he would become a licensed electrician and could go into business for himself. In fact, he spent so much time looking forward to it that he did not think much about his present job as an apprentice. He showed no initiative and had no interest in his work or his co-workers. Bruce felt he was a natural electrician, and so he did not bother much with routine things now. This job was just something to get through.

Bruce did exactly what he was told—no more, no less. Every day he had to be told again to do the same things. When the head electrician tried to talk to him, Bruce just said that he did not intend to spend his life working for that company. But he spent less time there than he had expected. He was fired after a few weeks. Though he may have been a good electrician, his attitude was poor.

Now Bruce may have had no intention of remaining an apprentice electrician all his life. It was all very well that he had ambition and plans. But his attitude hurt him. He concentrated so hard on the future that his attitude toward the present was poor. Although it is good to plan for the future, you cannot ignore the reality of the present. And your attitude will be judged and evaluated in the present, not the future. He did not realize that his becoming an electrician depended on his performance as an apprentice.

Your attitude determines whether you will have good human relations or poor, ineffective human relations. It determines how well you will succeed on a job. If you project a poor, indifferent, or negative attitude, you will have problems in dealing with others.

Project a Positive Attitude

If attitude is your state of mind—how you feel about things—what can you do if you do not like a situation or a person you must deal with? After all, Dulcie's and Bruce's attitudes only reflected how they really felt about things. What could they have done about that?

They could have realized two things: first, that if they did not change their basic attitudes, they probably would have unsatisfying careers, and, second, that they could have exercised some will power to project a different attitude.

The world will evaluate your attitude in terms of your behavior. Often it is necessary to behave differently from how you really want to at a given moment. If you do not do so, human relations problems may result. Sometimes, it suits your purpose to behave differently from how you would like.

You may say, "Well, if I behave differently from how I feel, isn't that somehow dishonest or not telling it like it is?" Not at all. In the first place, honesty or dishonesty is not involved. It is more a matter of acting with grace under pressure.

You might argue that the only "honest" behavior when you are feeling out of sorts is to let everyone know it, to be rude and to take out your unhappiness on others. But it is ridiculous to claim that it is dishonest to behave pleasantly toward others when you feel bad. It is as silly as saying that you are a dishonest football player if you continue to play with a painful, but minor, injury. You are not showing how you really feel, but you are displaying a positive attitude.

If you had a serious injury, though, you could not play football. You would be foolish to try. It is the same thing with your attitude. You can and should work to project a positive attitude, one that will balance your downs, or negative feelings. Just by smiling, some psychologists say, you will begin to feel better. You can work to change negative feelings so that you will be happier.

An attitude is not fixed forever in concrete. Nor do you have just one attitude. You have many attitudes, at different levels, and they change often. You have one attitude toward cars, another toward school, and so on. You like some people better than others, and your attitude shows it.

Attitudes are Self-Fulfilling

Taken together your attitudes reflect your essential character. How you feel about something at different times will be determined by your basic values, by your sense of identity, by your goals and how you feel you can achieve them. The basic theme that will run through all your attitudes can be characterized as either positive or negative. It is to your advantage to develop a positive attitude. After all, your attitude will pretty much determine what you get out of life and how you will be treated. Look at the two following cases:

Carla had a negative attitude toward school when she was there. She felt it was a waste of time. She got nothing out of it. Because of her negative attitude, she did not try hard. She ignored her assignments. She rarely read her textbooks. She seldom listened to the teachers. Not surprisingly, she got little in return. That strengthened her negative attitude and her belief that school was a waste of time.

Sylvia, on the other hand, was a naturally positive person. School was not her favorite part of life, but she had to go, and so she decided to get all she could from it. Sylvia had a positive attitude. She listened. She read. She thought about things. Sure enough, she got something for her effort—just as she had expected. Her experience strengthened her positive attitude.

Carla and Sylvia were experiencing a *self-fulfilling prophecy*—that is, they each got what they had expected out of school. Self-fulfilling prophecies affect much of one's life. People get what they expect, most of the time. And that is why a positive attitude is important.

Attitudes are Contagious

An important thing about your attitude is that it will spread. It is contagious. If you display a positive attitude, you will find that you usually are surrounded by other people with positive attitudes. The same applies if you have a negative attitude—you will be surrounded by negative people much of the time.

There is no magic involved in this. It is how things work, and it is easy to understand. Consider the case of Alexander:

Every morning Alexander's boss came into the office looking sour and angry. He ignored Alexander. He then would work until the coffee break, when he sometimes would come out and talk with one or two other workers. Alexander was upset by this behavior. He felt that the boss was ignoring him on purpose. But he did not try to speak with his boss. Alexander thought it was the boss's place to speak first.

The company had a policy that supervisors were to evaluate the performance of all employees once a year. Alexander's boss gave him high ratings for the quality of his work, but low ones for his attitude. When Alexander questioned this, the boss said he was snobby and unfriendly.

Alexander was surprised and somewhat resentful. When he asked for some examples, the boss said, "Well, when I come in in the morning, you never say anything. Also, when I join the other workers for a coffee break, you never join in."

Alexander left the meeting with mixed feelings. But he decided to try to change. His attitude had been that the boss should speak first. Now he was determined to be more outgoing, and his attitude reflected

it. He made a point of greeting the boss each morning. To his surprise, it seemed to change his own mood as well. Most work days became more pleasant.

A pleasant, positive attitude usually will pay off for you. If you give someone else a lift during the day, they probably will respond to you in the same way.

Your Behavior Reflects Your Attitudes

As you have already read, others will interpret your attitude in terms of your behavior. If you are always late for work, your super-

There are several common behavioral clues that people use to classify attitudes. It is worth your while to learn the characteristics associated with a positive attitude. If you have a positive attitude, you probably display them naturally. But if you have bad moods or have to force yourself to overcome a negative attitude, knowing the positive behavior characteristics can help you. Here are some characteristics of a positive attitude. How many can you honestly find in yourself?

- willingness to change
- willingness to see the other side
- not complaining or making excuses
- pleasant, friendly expression
- readiness to accept responsibility for errors
- not critical of others
- many interests
- respect for others

visor is going to decide that you do not have the right attitude.

If you complain a lot, do not show initiative, and seem sour all the time, people are going to say that you have a negative attitude.

Remember that you are always communicating when you are with other people. Based on what you communicate, people will decide whether you have a positive attitude or a negative one.

Sometimes what they decide may be different from what you feel. Remember that you can send false messages without realizing it.

Make Your Attitude Constructive

A good attitude is more than smiling at people and being polite or always looking on the bright side. These are all part of a positive attitude, but for effective human relations, your attitude must also be constructive.

A constructive attitude reflects a willingness to help, to be of assistance, to solve problems, to get the job done. Being positive and constructive work together to generate excellent human relations.

A surly person who is competent and provides good service to customers, for example, will make them uncomfortable and unwilling to do business with that person.

On the other hand, a person who is not competent or ready to help out when necessary, will not have good human relations, no matter how pleasant or smiling he or she is. Have a positive and a constructive attitude.

Be Aware of Your Attitude

Although most people tend to have a positive attitude, you cannot take that attitude for granted. When you face problems and have difficult times, it is all too easy to develop a negative attitude toward life. That is when you must be on guard. If you often find yourself showing a negative attitude, it is time to count your blessings and use your will power. Study the list of positive characteristics and try to behave as they suggest. A positive attitude will build good human relations and make your career satisfying.

Name _____   Date _____

Check Your Understanding

As you have learned, people's behavior often gives clues about their attitudes. By watching what they do, you can learn whether they have a positive or a negative attitude. In the same way, your own behavior will tell you things about yourself. Learn to identify your behavior as positive or negative. Then you can improve your attitude and your human relations.

In the situations below, people display behavior that is either positive or negative. Read each statement. Select the phrase on the left that best describes the behavior . Write the phrase number in the space provided at the right. Then characterize the behavior as positive or negative by writing a P or an N. After you have completed the exercise, compare your answers with those in the answer key on the last page of this chapter.

1. Criticizes others

2. Complains or makes excuses

3. Willing to change

4. Not critical of others

5. Accepts responsibility for errors

6. Unwilling to change

a. "Oh, I'm afraid that was all my fault," Marcie a. _____ said when the supervisor asked who had left the cover off the computer keyboard.

b. "Okay," Franco said, "I never thought of doing b. _____ it that way before. I'll try it."

c. "Betty never does her fair share. And I don't think c. _____ Terry tries as hard as he should," Marlene said. "And if you ask me, I'd say that he never should have been promoted."

d. "Well, I think Betty does excellent work. She d. _____ may be slower, but she is very accurate. I think she deserves credit."

e. "I didn't know we had to do it that way . It's not e. _____ my fault. No one told me. Besides, I have to do all the hard jobs," Chris said.

f. "We tried to do it that way at the last company I f. _____ worked for, and it backfired. I'm not saying it won't work here, but if it were my company, I'd do it just the way we always have. Why look for unnecessary trouble?"

Case Study

In the situation below, there is a human relations problem. Read about it and then answer the questions to solve the problem. Write your answers in the space provided.

"I don't think I can do that," Ann said. "I never really worked on projects that large."

"Of course you can, Ann," her supervisor, Ms. Choi, said. "It's just like the work you have been doing."

"Gee, I don't know. I'd rather not take the chance. I'm sure I'll get it wrong," Ann insisted.

"Well, OK. I'll get someone else to do it," Ms. Choi said.

Ann worked as a layout designer for a publishing company. Her job was to design attractive booklets and brochures. She did the work well, but she was unsure of herself. Several times Ms. Choi asked Ann to try larger, harder projects. Each time Ann said she did not think she could do them.

Once Ms. Choi was going on vacation and asked Ann to be acting supervisor. "Oh, I couldn't do that," Ann said. "I've never supervised other people before." "Nonsense," Ms. Choi said. "I'm sure you can do it. And it's only for one week. It will be good training for you."

"Oh no, I'd be terrible," Ann said. "I'd really rather not."

Ms. Choi asked another person to be the acting supervisor. Soon she stopped trying to get Ann to work on the larger, more important projects. Later, when Ms. Choi and the general manager were discussing people to promote to assistant supervisor, Ann's name came up.

"Well, I used to think that Ann showed a lot of promise," Ms. Choi said. "But I've changed my mind. I don't think she could do it. She's not a very positive person."

Case Study Analysis

a. What is the real problem?_____

_____

_____

b. What are the important facts to consider in this problem?_____

_____

_____

_____

_____

c. What solutions to this problem can you think of? Describe a few. _____

_____

_____

_____

_____

Name _____   Date _____

d. What would happen if the solutions you suggested were followed? Explain the results of each solution you described._____

_____

_____

_____

_____

e. Of the solutions you described, which would you recommend? Why? _____

_____

_____

_____

_____

Personal Assessment

There is always something to learn in the world around you. You can use this knowledge now, for instance, to identify positive and negative behavior traits, as well as your feelings toward people who display them.

From the people you know, pick two you like a lot and two you would rather not deal with. Label the ones you like "Person A" and "Person B." Label the ones you dislike "Person C" and "Person D." In the space provided below, list the characteristics each person displays. Think of why you like or dislike them. Are they fun to be around? Are they helpful? Do they make you feel good? At the end of each list, write down whether that person displays a positive attitude or a negative one. Compare your lists with those of your classmates and together make a list of all the positive traits and all the negative traits that you have identified.

Person A:_____

_____

_____

_____

_____

_____

_____

_____

_____

_____

Person B: _____

_____

_____
_____
_____
_____
_____
_____
_____
_____
_____

Person C: _____
_____
_____
_____
_____
_____
_____
_____
_____
_____
_____

Person D: _____
_____
_____
_____
_____
_____
_____
_____
_____
_____
_____

Answers to Check Your Understanding: a. 5, P; b. 3, P; c. 1, N; d. 4, P; e. 2, N; f. 6, N.

Chapter 11

HUMAN RELATIONS AND MORALE

After completing this chapter, you will be able to:

➤ *Recognize the connections among needs, motivation, and behavior.*

➤ *Identify the needs that motivate you.*

People act in certain ways because their needs, wants, and values propel them to do so. These propelling forces are called *motives*. A motive can be described as the reason why you do things. But motivation is more complicated than that.

Even experts disagree about precisely what motivates people to do things. There are many theories about what motivation is, and about what motivates people. Most theories agree on two facts, however, that indicate motivation:

1. Motivated people are energized; they have a higher energy level than unmotivated people.

2. Motivated people channel their increased energy toward specific goals.

For example, if you are motivated and set a goal to improve your grade in mathematics by ten points by the end of the semester, you would devote your increased energy to studying mathematics and doing mathematical problems.

It would not help much if you used your increased motivation and higher energy level to run faster in gym class. It may improve your gym grade, but would do little to improve your math test scores. So, motivation is goal-oriented.

Your will to work depends upon your motivation. The greater your motivation, the greater, in general, your will to work. You probably have heard people say of hard workers, "They are highly motivated." Motivation differs from person to person, but all people are motivated by the desire to satisfy their physical as well as psychological needs.

People try to satisfy their different needs at different times and in different ways. For some people, the needs for self-esteem and fulfillment can be met only by getting lots and lots of money.

Other people have a greater need for affection, and so they will give up money and make other sacrifices for the sake of having friends. Still others desire power to satisfy their need for fulfillment.

You can be a more efficient worker and have better human relations when you know what motivates you and when you understand what motivates others. If you are eating because you are hungry, you know what physical need you are satisfying. When psychological needs motivate you, unless you think about it, you might not always be aware of what need you are really trying to satisfy.

The Motivation and Behavior of Others

For good human relations, it helps to know what motivates other people in any given situation. Knowing this can often help you understand another person's behavior. And when you understand that, you are less likely to be annoyed by it or to cause that person to be annoyed.

If you were the manager of a plant, you might not care about the workers' motivation as long as they did their work. Well, that might be OK up to a point. But suppose that, by not understanding their motivation, you took steps that weakened or destroyed it. You would be destroying their will to work as well. And you would not be an effective manager. Consider this case:

Doug owned a small construction company that built homes. He employed four workers. At first, the crew worked hard and willingly. They showed they enjoyed their work, and they did a lot of it. Doug never tried to learn what motivated them. He was happy that they worked so hard. He assumed they were motivated by the desire to earn money.

Everyone who bought one of Doug's houses was pleased. The construction was excellent. Doug had no trouble selling all the houses he could build because word of their high quality spread.

Then Doug had what he thought was a brilliant idea: If he could build more houses, he would make more money. Doug told his workers that he would pay bonuses whenever they could do more work than usual in a day. The bonuses would be individual so the workers would compete for them. Those who worked hardest would get the most money.

For a few weeks, the plan seemed to work. More work was done. Then something began to happen. First the crew seemed to become less friendly and to enjoy their work less. Then the quality of their work dropped. Doug offered more bonuses, but things got worse. Then one worker quit, and another one threatened to.

Finally, Doug realized that his workers had not been motivated only by money. They wanted fair pay, of course. But before Doug introduced the elements of competition and speed, the workers had enjoyed each other and had taken pride in doing quality work. Not knowing what motivated them, Doug had undermined their will to work by mistakenly thinking that money alone was their motivation.

Now you will not own a company, or even be a supervisor, right away. Still, it is important for you to know that people have different motivations for working. Knowing this can help you build and maintain good human relations.

If you know that one of your co-workers takes pride in the work itself, you are not likely to offend that person by talking as if only money mattered. And if you know another co-worker is interested only in money, you will not waste your time talking about the work itself with that person.

Motivation and Behavior

Knowing about your own motivation is important too. Surprisingly, your own motives are not always clear even to yourself. They depend on your values and the goals you set for yourself—after, of course, you have satisfied your physical needs.

Some people are not highly motivated. They are happy simply to earn a decent living in order to have food, clothes, and a roof over their heads. There is nothing wrong with that. They do their work well enough to keep their jobs, and they are unlikely to become bored. They know that they are working to meet their needs.

Other people are highly motivated. They try to get increasingly important jobs or to do increasingly better work. Such people are said to have *aspirations*—that is, high goals or high hopes. One aspires to be the president of the union or the supervisor or the division manager. One hopes to do the best job that has ever been done.

Young people just starting out on their careers generally have high goals. Older workers either have attained their goals or have had to settle for something less than what they had wanted.

Some people set unrealistic goals and later suffer because they do not reach them. It is important to spend time deciding who you are and what your values are to set realistic goals.

After you have reached your goals, you still can get satisfaction from doing your job well. This satisfaction will do much to help you avoid the boredom that many workers face in their later years.

The more realistically you have chosen your goals and identified your aspirations, the less likely you are to become bored at your work.

Motivation Outside of Work

The likelihood of becoming bored with your work is real, even under the best conditions. A protection against boredom is a full, satisfying life away from the job. Hobbies and other interests that provide outside motivation are important.

Many people are strongly motivated at work by their outside interests. They are willing to work hard to earn money or time off so they can spend it on hobbies outside of work. There is nothing wrong with that. No one said that a person should live only to work. In fact, the more sensible course is to work in order to live an interesting life.

For some people, a job is less important than a hobby.

Alisha, for example, was interested in skin diving and surfing. She took jobs waiting on tables at resorts where she could pursue these hobbies. She would work in the north during the summer and move south in the winter.

Benji followed a similar plan. He liked to ski. He used his skills as a carpenter to find jobs at ski resorts, and he moved around with the ski season.

People like Alisha and Benji are highly motivated, but their motivation comes from outside their work. However, you need to make your work enough of a priority so it is done well and you can concentrate on it while you are doing it. You need to find a balance of work and outside activities. Remember Dulcie of Chapter 10, whose social life was too important to her and who had a bad attitude toward her job.

Different Motivation Patterns

Although it often may seem difficult to understand your own motivations, much less the motivations of others, some understanding of what motivates others will help you to maintain good human relations. People seem to follow patterns that can serve as hints about their motivation. Be careful using these clues. Remember that generalizations can be misleading.

With that in mind, consider the following motivation patterns.

Finished-Job Pattern

People who have a *finished-job pattern* desire to finish a job for its own sake. They work hard to achieve a feeling of accomplishment. They could be satisfying a need for fulfillment or recognition—an outside observer can only guess which one.

But the important point here is that, for such people, the sense of accomplishment that comes from doing a job well is more important than money. Doug's construction workers had this motivation. If Doug had recognized the pattern, he would not have thought that personal bonuses would generate more work.

Friendship Pattern

People who make every effort to be liked and to be surrounded by friends are said to display the *friendship pattern*. Such people probably are fulfilling their needs for affection and recognition. They have a problem, though, in balancing their need for friends against other values.

For example, many workers may compromise some of their principles and even their self-respect for the sake of remaining friendly with co-workers. They may keep quiet to avoid problems. Such people run this risk: To keep from rocking the boat, they never get it away from the shore. Sometimes it is necessary to take a stand that can be difficult if you are ruled by the need to be liked.

Perfection Pattern

People who are more interested in the technical aspects of a job rather than in their co-workers or in finishing a task show this pattern of behavior. Such people value excellence. They usually strive for professional growth and mastery of a job. These things mean more to them than money, friendship, or the final completion of a task. And once the task is completed, these people will push on to the next task and try to do it perfectly too.

Power Pattern

Some people are motivated by a desire for power. Such people often make excellent leaders and will usually perform best in a situation when their role as leader is emphasized. A possible problem with such people, however, is that they may choose to retain control at the expense of productivity.

Patterns Change

Some people may follow two or more of these motivation patterns, but usually one pattern will rule a person's life. You can use the pattern as a clue to understanding the motivation of others. But remember that it is dangerous to generalize about people. Remember too that people's needs—and thus their motivations—change.

Needs Influence Motivation

Everyone is motivated in some way or another by one thing or another. If you hear someone say that another person has no motivation at all and just does not care about work, do not believe it. The person may not be motivated to do a particular job. But that person does have other motivations.

Basically, people are motivated to satisfy their most pressing need first. If they are hungry, they will be motivated to eat. If they are tired, they will sleep. When they try to satisfy their psychological needs, they seem to follow the same pattern. That is, they are motivated by the need they feel most strongly.

For example, a person who has never had to worry about money usually will not be strongly motivated by a desire to earn money and for security. Instead, the need for affection might be stronger, especially if the person had been given little affection early in life.

Your Values Motivate You

Your *values* also motivate you. Values, like personality and behavior, are shaped by your environment. Six values that influence motivation are:

1. *Achievement*—people value achievements and have higher motivation in jobs that offer the opportunity to achieve something.

2. *Altruism*—people value helping others and being of service to others.

3. *Autonomy*—people value a degree of independence and a chance to offer ideas and initiate activities.

4. *Comfort*—people value a comfortable work place, with low *stress* and pleasant working conditions.

5. *Safety*—people value order and predictability in their work lives. They want to feel that their jobs are safe.

6. *Status*—people value recognition and the feeling that their job is an important and respected one.

Different people place different priorities on these values. Someone who values autonomy more than achievement may choose a job where the chance for promotion is low, but where he can set his own hours and make own decisions. Someone who highly values safety would not become a fire fighter, no matter how well the job might pay. The values you give priority to, along with your needs and your individual personality, will motivate you in your job.

Motivation and Career Choices

To make the right career choice, you should be aware of your needs and understand your motivation. People do not perform well if they do not choose careers that reflect their motivation.

Motivation affects your desire to learn new skills. If you are interested in learning a skill, you will learn faster and better than you will if you are not interested. Your interest is often determined by the same factors that motivate you to study in class or perform well on the job.

Motives are not always benign or positive. Some people may be motivated to behave antisocially. For example, they will cheat on exams to get good grades, or they will steal company secrets to sell to a competitor to profit financially. The important thing to remember is that although your motives influence your behavior, you decide how you will act.

Motivation may be indirect—as in the person who works hard to support an outside hobby—but there is a connection between motivation and career.

Name _____   Date _____

Check Your Understanding

1. A good way to recognize your needs is to analyze the actions of others to guess what motivates them. Doing this will often provide clues about your own motivations. In the situations below, decide whether the person is highly or poorly motivated. If highly motivated, try to identify the need(s) that the individual may be trying to satisfy: physical (such as getting money for food, clothing, shelter), psychological (such as affection, esteem, self-fulfillment), or both. If you think the person is poorly motivated, you do not have to identify any need. Check the appropriate space. After you have completed the exercise, compare your answers with those in the answer key on the last page of this chapter.

a. Sheri's family was well off. She always had money to buy what she wanted and needed as she was growing up. Her parents were busy people. Both of them had careers, and they were away from home a lot. Sheri spent little time with them. She often felt lonely. She also felt that she did not measure up to her parents.
Highly motivated _____   Poorly motivated _____
Physical needs_____   Psychological needs _____

b. Rubi lived her life from day to day. She was an attractive, friendly person who collected admirers easily. She had not developed any particular goals and was content to drift along enjoying the pleasures of the moment.
Highly motivated _____   Poorly motivated _____
Physical needs_____   Psychological needs _____

c. Bud's family was never well off. They lived in a poor section of town, and both parents had to work hard to buy the essential food and clothes and pay the rent. However, they managed to spend a lot of time with Bud. They encouraged him in his interests, they showed him affection, and they give him a lot of praise.
Highly motivated _____   Poorly motivated _____
Physical needs_____   Psychological needs _____

d. Jorge was the youngest of six children. His older brothers and sisters had gone to prestigious colleges. When he was in high school, his parents lost their jobs. He had to work to help support the family and to have a chance of going to college like his brothers and sisters.
Highly motivated _____   Poorly motivated _____
Physical needs_____   Psychological needs _____

2. You read that six values motivate workers. Match the values to their definitions and to the correct examples in the following table. After you have completed the exercise, compare your answers with those in the answer key on the last page of this chapter.

Values	Definitions	Examples
1. achievement	a. accomplishing something	i. It was important to Becca to work in a quiet office with cheerful people. 1. _____
2. altruism	b. a setting with little stress and pleasant conditions	ii. Bill liked working for himself because he decided how much to charge. 2. _____
3. autonomy	c. order and predictability	iii. Jacqui went into politics so she would be admired and could do something essential for society 3. _____
4. comfort	d. helping and being of service	iv. Kevin looked forward to finishing the filming of the movie 4. _____
5. safety	e. recognition and respect	v. Sam said he did not like change. He enjoyed knowing that his company would be around long into the future. 5. _____
6. status	f. acting on one's own ideas and opinions	vi. Johanna was a social worker with the poorest of the poor and helped people get money for food. 6. _____

Case Study

In the situation below, there is a human relations problem. Read about it and then answer the questions to solve the problem. Write your answers in the space provided.

When she graduated from high school, Elaine went to work at Golden's, a large department store in a nearby city. She did not think much about the job one way or the other. She knew she had to have a job, and a lot of her friends worked there.

Elaine worked as a salesperson in the home furnishings department. For the first few weeks, it was somewhat interesting. At least it was different from school. But after a short time, Elaine became bored with it.

"You just stand around all day," she complained to a co-worker, Theo. "Wait on the dumb customers and that's it."

Theo said he rather liked it. "It's fun helping people find what they need to furnish a house or apartment," he explained. "I hope to be manager some day and perhaps have my own store."

"How can anyone find furniture interesting?" Elaine asked with a sigh.

"Well, what would you like to do?" Theo asked.

"Oh, I don't know. Anything but this, I guess," Elaine said. Elaine's lack of interest communicated itself to customers. Many of them would try to get Theo to wait on them rather than Elaine. Since the salespersons earned commissions on sales, Elaine did not make as much money as Theo. This annoyed her. She thought it was not fair. It also made her even more dissatisfied with what she was doing.

Elaine began to come to work late. She often called in sick when she "just couldn't face another day of boring work."

Name _____   Date _____

Case Study Analysis

a. What is the real problem? _____
_____
_____

b. What are the important facts to consider in this problem? _____
_____
_____
_____

c. What solutions to this problem can you think of? Describe a few. _____
_____
_____
_____

d. What would happen if the solutions you suggested were followed? Explain the results of each solution you described. _____
_____
_____
_____

e. Of the solutions you described, which would you recommend? Why? _____
_____
_____
_____

Personal Assessment

If you can identify what motivates you, you will be able to set realistic goals and work toward them to satisfy your needs. One good way to do this is to study the life of someone whom you admire. It can be someone from any period of history and any country. Pick someone and read books or articles about this person.

On a separate sheet of paper, write a brief report about the person's life. Tell what you admire about this person and try to identify what motivated her or him to be successful. Answer the following questions in your report: What needs was the person attempting to satisfy? Where did these needs come from? How did this person satisfy these needs? Was this person always successful in satisfying these needs? Share your report with your classmates. As a group, decide which person reported on had the strongest motivation. Why did you think so?

Answers to Check Your Understanding: 1 a. Highly motivated, psychological needs; b. Poorly motivated; c. Highly motivated, physical needs; d. Poorly motivated. 2 1., a., iv; 2., d., vi; 3., f., ii; 4., b., i; 5., c., v; 6., e., iii.

Chapter 12

MOTIVATION AND MORALE

After completing this chapter, you will be able to:

➤ *Identify causes of low morale.*

➤ *Recognize connections among satisfaction, morale, and motivation.*

➤ *Analyze the morale and motivation of yourself and others.*

If you enjoy your work, you will have high morale. If you do not enjoy your work, you will have low morale. Satisfaction comes from a sense that your job is worthwhile and you do it well.

People like to feel important and that what they do is essential. Some workers have jobs that seem unimportant. They cannot see how what they do makes a difference. They do not feel that they are doing something worthwhile. Such workers derive little job satisfaction, no matter how well motivated.

Morale grows out of job satisfaction. Where there is high morale, there are good human relations. Where morale is low, human relations suffer.

Motivation Affects Morale

Without motivation you will have little job satisfaction. This will hold true no matter how high your pay or how pleasant your surroundings. Does this mean that job satisfaction and morale depend completely upon your own motivation? Happily, they do not.

Although it is true that you must be motivated to have job satisfaction and high morale, these things will not automatically follow high motivation. Other factors influence how you feel and the satisfaction you get from your work.

Two major influences affect your job satisfaction and morale: your own motivation—what you bring to the job—and your job environment. You read about motivation in the last chapter. Now you will look at environmental factors that are important to your sense of job satisfaction.

Your Work Environment Affects Your Morale

Your pay, your physical surroundings, your co-workers, your supervisors, and company policies all affect your morale.

Pay

Pay is important to you for many reasons. First of all, of course, you need a certain amount of money simply to live. You must buy food, clothes, and shelter. You also will want money to buy some of life's pleasures, such as a nice car, an evening at the movies, or dinner out.

These are practical reasons why your pay is important. But it is important in another way too. Pay is a measure of success and status. To some extent, the higher your pay, the greater your success. Your pay helps you meet your many needs of all levels.

For these reasons, your salary has a direct effect on your morale. Your primary motivation may not be to make money, but if you do not get enough of it, your morale will be affected.

Physical Surroundings

Your physical surroundings affect your morale. If you work in a dirty, crowded, dark, poorly ventilated place, your morale will suffer no matter how well motivated you are. There are some things you can expect your company to do to protect your safety and health. Tell your supervisor about conditions that keep you from performing well, such as poor lighting or uncomfortable temperatures.

Relationships with Co-Workers

Your morale can be affected by your relationship with co-workers. For this reason, good human relations is important. Sometimes, there is little you can do to change an unpleasant co-worker into a pleasant one. But few people are unpleasant all the time. As you have learned, you can improve your own human relations to make friends or, at least, acceptable companions of most co-workers.

You do not need to feel that the people at work are your best friends. They do not need to have the same backgrounds and values that you do. It takes all kinds of people to make the world an interesting place, and at work you will meet many of these people. Perhaps the most important rule in dealing with others is not to judge them by your own standards of behavior. After all, do you want others to judge you by their individual—and differing—standards? There is room in the work place, and the world, for people of different values, talents, and abilities.

Remember, your co-workers will react to you as you react to them. Keep the lines of communication open and you will enhance your relationships with your co-workers.

Relationships with Supervisors

Another factor that influences your morale is the type of supervision you receive. If your supervisor overuses his or her parent self and always orders you about, your morale will suffer. Your morale will suffer if the supervisor always ignores or criticizes you.

You bear the primary responsibility for maintaining good relationships with your co-workers. These are your horizontal relationships. Your supervisor is primarily responsible for the quality of the relationship between you. Relation-ships between two work levels are vertical relationships. Supervisors decide the tone of the work place, and how formal or informal relationships will be.

Many companies have interpersonal training for their managers. Most supervisors want to foster good relationships with their staff, because they know that this helps morale. Happy workers are often more productive and productive workers make managers look good.

Company Policies

Company policies and the benefits you receive in addition to pay will affect your morale. While neutral policies will have little effect on morale, policies that damage or help you have an effect on your morale. This is true of all external conditions that affect your morale. For most workers, external conditions will neither be very bad nor exceptionally good. Most companies will do all they can to make external conditions favorable.

For your peace of mind—and to improve your relations with others—realize that you are not the only one responsible for your morale. It can, and probably will, be affected by external conditions.

Morale Changes Over Time

Another thing you should know about morale is that it will change. Changes in morale may not relate directly to anything—neither to external conditions nor to internal motivation. This is normal.

Psychologists who study morale changes have determined that most people swing through a cycle during their working lives. When they first start to work, they tend to have high morale.

They look forward to their new life and to the opportunities it presents. After about a year, this enthusiasm weakens, and so does their morale.

After around two years on the same job, a worker's morale is likely to be low in comparison to what it was at first. How low it goes depends upon the individual worker's motivation, as well as upon external conditions at work. But regardless of all these factors, morale tends to dip even lower after about the third year. Many workers change jobs after three or four years.

If you experience this slump in morale, do not despair. There does not seem to be any real reason for it. Studies of workers have shown that after about five years, morale and interest begin to pick up again—even though job conditions and pay are not much different from what they were during the low period.

This change in morale happens because, after five years on the job, workers will tend to change some of their goals. Consciously or not, they try to evaluate what they want. If necessary, they may lower their goals as a realistic adjustment to their lives and careers. In addition, after five years, workers have learned their jobs well enough to feel confident. They have learned how to get along with their co-workers—even with those few who create problems— and they feel accepted.

Raise Your Morale

Be prepared for your morale to be low at times. Then, be especially careful about your human relations. When your morale is low, you are likely to be annoyed easily, to be unfriendly, even rude. At such times, you must control yourself when dealing with your co-workers and supervisors. If your morale does sink, try to find out why as quickly and objectively as you can. Some guidelines follow.

Consider Your Motivation

Many workers are quick to blame the company when things do not go right. Consider that possibility, but do not deceive yourself. If the fault is your own, changing jobs will not correct it, and you will be disappointed. And your career will go nowhere. Louis was a case in point:

Louis has had three different jobs in four years, and was about to change jobs again. He never felt any job satisfaction; his morale was low. He blamed this on the companies he worked for. He felt that no one understood him. And so Louis moved from company to company. He was always employed as a mail clerk.

Louis did not want to be a mail clerk. He had drifted into it. Because he did not value his job, he never bothered to learn the company procedures affecting it. He figured it did not matter. When supervisors tried to tell Louis how the company wanted the work done, he would say, "Yeah," and promptly forget it.

Louis was annoyed much of the time because his supervisors always seemed to be picking on him. His morale stayed low. He kept changing jobs, hoping to find a supervisor who would not pick on him. Fortunately,

Louis began to realize that his problem stemmed from within himself—he lacked motivation. That discovery helped him to turn his life around. He began to work harder because he was motivated to get a better job—not one that only paid his way, but one that satisfied him.

If you suffer from low morale and are not getting any satisfaction out of your job, look at yourself realistically. Ask yourself two basic questions: (1) Am I doing what I really want to do?, and (2) Are my expectations too high?

Identify External Factors

If you know that you are not just in a down period and you feel that the problem does not lie within you, take steps to identify external factors that may keep you from having job satisfaction.

If something is bothering you, it is better to bring it into the open and talk about it than to bottle it up. If you try to hide your problems, they will grow inside you. Your morale may sink lower.

Ask your supervisor to set aside time for a talk. It is more productive to approach the supervisor this way, with some warning, than to rush in with your problem at a time when you are emotional.

Use your human relations skills when you meet. Describe the problem as clearly and honestly as you can, especially if you feel annoyed and unhappy. Avoid communication stoppers, such as making complaints about co-workers, supervisors, or the company. This is a good way to end communication. You want to start a conversation to discover what the problems are and how to solve them. Consider this example:

Stephanie Scott developed a morale problem. She worked as a legal secretary for five lawyers. She liked her work and was good at it. For a long time, her morale was high, and she got much satisfaction from her work. Then one of the lawyers was replaced by a new one, Selena Ming.

Selena's approach bothered Stephanie. She began to feel inefficient when Selena gave her detailed instructions. Selena would also say such things as, "Do you think I can have this by 5?"

That question annoyed Stephanie, because it was asked at 9 in the morning. Stephanie knew that she worked fast. She took Selena's question to mean that she could not finish the job in time. Stephanie began to think about finding another job. But there were many good things about her job, so Stephanie decided to tell Selena what was bothering her. She asked Selena for some time to talk. She would try to tell Selena what the job meant to her and how she felt.

Stephanie was wise. She began by telling Selena how much she liked her job. She said that a main reason she liked it was that she felt confident and able to do it well, and that the other lawyers seemed to agree. She then asked Selena whether she was doing anything wrong.

"Why, no," Selena said. "Your work is really excellent." Stephanie then asked why Selena gave so

many directions, even on the most routine jobs.

"I didn't realize I was doing that," Selena answered. *"I guess it's because I'm new here and I want to do everything right."*

"Also, I sometimes feel you don't think I will get your work done," Stephanie said. *"What on earth gives you that idea?"* Selena asked.

"Well, whenever you give me something—no matter how early in the day—you always ask whether I can finish it by 5 o'clock."

"That's just my way of apologizing for giving you so much work," Selena explained. *"I certainly don't mean to suggest that you are at fault. Quite the opposite—you're very helpful to me. I'm sorry that those useless expressions have bothered you, and I'll try to avoid them from now on. Thanks for letting me know how you feel."*

Stephanie felt better. Her morale improved. She realized that Selena did respect her. A direct conversation is often the best way to solve problems.

Serious Problems

If an informal approach does not work, or if problems are more serious, you can take other steps to correct conditions. Most companies have grievance procedures to handle complaints and problems of employees. They provide you with a formal course of action to take to solve problems.

The procedures usually require a complaint to be in writing, and they often involve a hearing before company representatives. If you are in a union, its representatives may also be involved.

Grievance procedures are used to correct serious offenses. They are used when the company or its representative violates a work contract, a fair labor law, or health and safety standards.

Formal grievance procedures do not deal with minor problems that develop in the daily give-and-take of a worker's life, no matter how badly they may affect your morale. You can solve these problems on your own, as Stephanie did, by effective human relations.

No Job Is Perfect

Only as a last resort should you quit. If you are mistaken about the cause of your problem—if it is in you, not in the job—you will take your problem with you. Even if your problem is caused by the job environment, it is often best to try to solve it where you are. Remember that few jobs are perfect—all have their problems. Quitting a job is the last resort, the solution when all else fails.

Name _____   Date _____

Check Your Understanding

When you suffer from low morale, it is sometimes difficult to identify your problems. A good way to develop that skill is to look at another person's situation and see how it relates to morale and job satisfaction. Read the work situations described below. Decide whether the worker's morale is high or low and whether the source of the worker's morale is the result of internal or external conditions, or both. Place a check mark in the appropriate columns on the right. After you have completed the exercise, compare your answers with those in the answer key on the last page of this chapter.

		Morale		Source	
		High	*Low*	*Internal*	*External*
a.	Jayne worked in a crowded, overheated office. The lighting was not good, and she often felt her eyes were strained. The ventilation was poor, and so the air was often stuffy. Jayne did like the kind of work she was doing, and she was good at it.				
b.	Katrina's job was demanding physically. She was a carpenter's apprentice and had to carry heavy building materials. But Katrina loved hard physical work, and she looked forward to the day when she would be a journeyman carpenter. Her boss taught her the skills she needed and was always quick to praise her.				
c.	Manny worked in a beautiful new building as an insurance policy writer. The company provided a nice cafeteria, short working hours, and two breaks during the day. Manny's boss was easy to work with, and his co-workers were friendly. Yet Manny spent a lot of time daydreaming about his secret desire to be an airplane pilot.				
d.	Jacob worked in a social welfare agency. The job was demanding, the hours were long, and the pay was low. He had to deal with all kinds of people. But helping people made him feel good, and whenever a person thanked him, Jacob felt especially happy.				
e.	Gerri really liked her job. She was good at it, and she knew it. She willingly worked long hours and took on extra duties whenever the company had a problem. However, the company took Gerri for granted. Her pay raises were few and far between, and she got little praise.				

Case Study

In the situation below, there is a human relations problem. Read about it and then answer the questions to solve the problem. Write your answers in the space provided.

Kirsten was happy when she began working as a camera operator on the news program for a local television station. She had planned and studied to be a television camera operator for as long as she could remember.

Kirsten was eager to learn more on the job and to develop her talent. Her own happiness made her overlook the fact that some of the other camera operators at the station seemed less than happy and enthusiastic.

Soon, though, Kirsten began to realize that something was wrong and that her job was not going to be the joy that she had believed it would be. Hal Petrarca, the station manager, turned out to be a difficult person to work with. For one thing, he never praised the operators' work. No matter what Kirsten shot, he would say she should have done it differently.

Kirsten covered a fire, and Hal criticized her for not showing more of the crowd watching it. The next time she covered a fire, she made a point of showing the crowd. Hal said that she should have concentrated on the fire.

Later she began to realize that Pedro, another camera operator, was getting all the best assignments. She and the others covered routine stories. Pedro covered the exciting ones and the big ones. Also, Pedro was allowed to think up and shoot his own feature stories. No one else was.

When Kirsten asked for special assignments, Hal said, "No, you're not ready."

Kirsten tried to do some stories on her own. Hal never used them. He also continued to find fault with everything that she did. It was not long before Kirsten's enthusiasm for her career began to weaken. She even began to think that she should look into another line of work.

Case Study Analysis

a. What is the real problem?_____

_____

_____

b. What are the important facts to consider in this problem?_____

_____

_____

_____

c. What solutions to this problem can you think of? Describe a few. _____

_____

_____

_____

Name _____   Date _____

d. What would happen if the solutions you suggested were followed? Explain the results of each solution you described._____

_____

_____

_____

e. Of the solutions you described, which would you recommend? Why? _____

_____

_____

_____

Personal Assessment

In this chapter, you have looked at morale and job satisfaction from the worker's point of view. But employers are also concerned with morale. In this exercise you will learn what companies do to help keep morale high. Pick two companies near you. Visit or write a letter to the personnel director. Ask the director what the company does to maintain morale. Record your findings in the space provided below.

a. Company/personnel director: _____

Measures to improve morale: _____

_____

_____

_____

_____

b. Company/personnel director: _____

Measures to improve morale: _____

_____

_____

_____

_____

Next pick two workers who have been working for at least three years. They do not have to work at either of the companies you are investigating. Ask them what factors have helped keep their morale and job satisfaction high, and what factors have hurt their morale. Record your findings in the space provided below.

c. Worker/company:_____

Factors helping morale:_____

_____

_____

_____

_____

Factors hurting morale: _____

_____

_____

_____

_____

_____

d. Worker/company:_____

Factors helping morale:_____

_____

_____

_____

_____

Factors hurting morale: _____

_____

_____

_____

_____

Compare the workers' reactions with your own reactions. On the basis of this, answer the questions below in the space provided.

1. What factors help your morale at work or at school?_____

_____

_____

_____

2. What factors hurt your morale? _____

_____

_____

_____

3. What needs provide the most motivation for you?_____

_____

_____

_____

Answers to Check Your Understanding: a. Low morale, external; b. High morale, internal, external; c. Low morale, internal; d. High morale, internal; e. High morale, internal.

Chapter 13

THE STRESSES OF WORK

After completing this chapter, you will be able to:

- ➤ *Recognize the causes of stress and its impact on your career, your home life, and your health.*

- ➤ *Recognize the special stresses caused by beginning a new job.*

- ➤ *Identify three major stress areas in your life.*

You prepare to begin a new job, take an important exam, go on a blind date, or make an expensive purchase. Before the event, you may find that your mind keeps returning to the upcoming event. You may have trouble sleeping as you anticipate what will happen. As you enter the door to the job, class, blind date, or store, you may find that your heart is pounding, your throat is dry, and you feel jittery or jumpy with nervous energy—the butterflies-in-your-stomach feeling. You are experiencing the physical symptoms of stress—a sense of emotional disruption.

Everyone Encounters Stress

Everyone feels stress at one time or another. You may even feel stress at happy times—the birth of a child, getting the promotion you wanted, being elected class president. Life would be pretty boring if every day was the same as the one before, with no stress and no excitement. But all changes in life—good and bad—are accompanied by stress.

Stress can be good and useful. It is not always a bad thing. If you did not feel stress before a test, you might not study, and might fail the test. At work, some stress may cause you to try harder and improve your productivity, and thus your chances for career success.

Stress Levels Vary

Different careers have different stress levels. Compare the stress level felt by a cashier facing a long line of customers with that of a fire fighter rushing into a burning building, or an airline pilot responsible for landing a crippled jet safely. All three face stress, but the degree of stress is different. So is the constancy.

A cashier may face a long line of customers several times a day; the airline pilot may face a dangerous situation only once in his or her career. Both, however, must be prepared to deal with the stresses inherent in their particular job.

Work produces stress because it plays such an important role in everyone's life. Work helps you support yourself and your family, not only physically, through wages, but also emotionally, through increased self-esteem and pride in a job well done. Problems and challenges at work are magnified because of the importance of work in your life.

The Negative Side of Stress

Some stress may enhance performance. However, constant, unrelenting stress can have a negative effect on your mental and physical health. It can lead to poor performance at your job. Continuous stress can weaken your coping mechanisms and lead to inefficiency and low morale.

Continuous stress can also interfere with your personal life. Ideally, job stress would be left at work, and home would be a place for rest and relaxation. Unfortunately, we cannot shut off our minds that easily. Stress at work often leads to tension and anxiety off the job.

The reverse is also true. Worries about money, children, health, and other family matters may be stressful and carry over to your job performance. Add stress both at work and at home together, and you have too much stress. In the following example, Lisa faced too much stress as she tried to cope with pressures in and out of work.

Lisa could not believe that the job of her dreams was finally opening up. She had thought it would be years before she would be promoted to head air traffic controller. But Mrs. Chung had elected to take early retirement and travel, and Lisa was offered the position.

At first Lisa was elated. She knew that she deserved the promotion. Her work was excellent, her demeanor always professional. The increased salary was an important consideration as well. Lisa had enjoyed her shorter working days, however, and knew that Mrs. Chung was a demanding boss to work for.

Several days after Lisa was promoted, her baby-sitter quit. Lisa was stunned—with two preschoolers at home, good daycare was essential to her ability to do her job well. Her mother offered to help out, but she was planning a vacation to visit Lisa's sister across the country, and did not want to cancel her plans.

Between the stresses of work due to increased responsibility and a demanding new boss, and her worries about her children, Lisa felt as if she were running on a treadmill with no way to get off. She was short-tempered with her children and her co-workers. The job of her dreams was turning into a nightmare.

Workers who face prolonged periods of stress may find that their physical health is affected. Studies have shown that stress can reduce your body's defense mechanisms, resulting in more frequent or prolonged bouts of colds, flu, or depression.

After facing constant stress, workers may suffer from emotional exhaustion. This is called *burnout*. Burnout is common in jobs that require intense, constant performance and in which the worker has little control. Social workers and teachers are frequently victims of burnout.

Coping With Stress

Just reading about the negative effects of stress can be depressing. It may seem that stress is a factor beyond your control. This is the case many times. What you can control, however, is your response to stress.

People respond to stress in different ways. Some people react with anger and aggression. Others become fixated on one response, reacting in the same way to all stress, no matter what the source. Some people react in a childlike way—with a temper tantrum—when facing stress. This is called *regression*.

Some people prefer to pretend that the stress is not happening. They react by *denial*. They may escape into television, or reading. Other people may avoid the whole stressful situation. They refuse to deal with it by indefinitely postponing facing the situation. Withdrawal and avoidance can be even more harmful if they are accomplished through the use of alcohol or drugs.

The most effective way of coping with stress is to meet it head-on, recognize it, and resolve it if possible. In general, developing and practicing effective stress-reduction techniques can be helpful.

Stress Reduction

The first step in reducing stress is to identify the source of the stress. Is it external or internal? External stress may be beyond your control, but internal stress is something you can deal with. Are you pushing yourself to get ahead faster than your job situation or family situation will allow? Are you adding to your stress load by always expecting more, bigger, or better things from yourself? Do you expect to be perfect, and demand perfection from those around you?

These internal sources of stress, added to stress inherent in your job, can be crippling. Identifying them is the first step toward overcoming them.

Become a Problem-Solver

Being presented with a seemingly unsolvable problem—as Lisa was with her daycare dilemma—can be very stressful. Developing good problem-solving strategies can help you deal with stress. These are four steps to good problem-solving:

1. Identify the problem

2. Think of different solutions

3. Decide which solution is best for you

4. Review your solution and adjust it if necessary.

Tackling stressful problems in this systematic way will help you face problems head on, without avoidance.

It may help to brainstorm solutions with a relative, friend, or co-worker, or to write them out on paper. All perfec-

tionists should notice Step 4: it is not always possible to find the best solution to a problem the first time you try.

Do Not Go Looking for Stress

Life is stressful enough without putting yourself in situations that will increase your stress load. If you are overextended at work, do not volunteer to organize the company picnic. If your home life is hectic, do not plan the birthday party to end all parties for your spouse. Have a few friends over for a quiet celebration instead.

Avoid situations that are stressful for you, if you can do so without jeopardizing your career or home life. If calling on customers is part of your job description, but you get tense every time you must meet someone new, then perhaps you are in the wrong business.

Confront Stress

When you cannot avoid stress, your best bet may be to confront it. If you feel stressed because you have been passed up for a promotion several times, do not just feel bad about it. That is not productive. And do not avoid the situation—that certainly will not help. Instead, ask to speak to your supervisor about the reasons why you have been passed over.

If you dread meeting people, and this is a major obstacle in pursuing your dream career, confront your fear. Join a club, plan a way to meet people weekly or daily, or do whatever it takes to reduce your anxiety in unfamiliar situations.

Exercise Your Stress Away

Physical activity is a great stress-reducer. When you feel overloaded with stress, take an activity break. Walk, run, lift weights, swim, play golf or racquetball—whatever you enjoy that allows you to work off steam.

Coping With a New Job

One stress-provoking situation we all face is the stress of facing a new job. There are many reasons for this. One is that change is inherently stressful. Another reason is that most people want to do a good job; they want to prove to the employer that they are the right person for the job. They need to feel that they are capable. In a new job, with a new job description and unfamiliar duties, this usually takes time.

When beginning a new job, you need to adapt to a different way of doing things, different co-workers, and a different supervisor. There is usually a period of initiation—testing—to see if you are up to the group standards.

It is rare for a new employee to be immediately accepted into the group. It is far more common to experience some loneliness and uncertainty the first few days on a job.

Try to remember that this will pass. React with good humor to teasing, and you will be accepted by your peers. Ask intelligent questions as you learn your job, and you will be accepted by your supervisor.

Knowing that everyone faces this period of uncertainty may help you to cope with the stress of a new job.

Name _____   Date _____

Check Your Understanding

You have learned that there are two basic types of stress. **External** stress is often out of your control, but by recognizing that fact, you may be better able to cope with it. **Internal** stress is under your control. Problem-solving processes can help you cope with internal stress, or even eliminate it. Decide whether the examples of stress listed below are internal or external, or both. Place a check in the appropriate column. After you have completed the exercise, compare your answers with those in the answer key on the last page of this chapter.

	Cause of Stress	*Internal*	*External*
a.	Your father has suffered a stroke and is hospitalized.		
b.	A promotion at work increases your workload and your hours.		
c.	You have been assigned to a prestigious committee at work but are afraid you are not capable of performing well.		
d.	You win the lottery.		
e.	You are passed over for promotion.		
f.	You are planning to move across the country.		
g.	A major report is due and you are procrastinating about beginning it.		
h.	Your mother loses her job and becomes depressed.		
i.	You begin a new job.		

Case Study

In the situation below, there is a human relations problem. Read about it and then answer the questions to solve the problem. Write your answers in the space provided.

Life was going well for Malcolm. He had a nice apartment—although it was small—and a congenial roommate. He was active in the community adult sports league and coached Little League. He had a job he enjoyed in a sporting goods store and was going to school two nights a week to get his college degree.

When Malcolm arrived at work Monday, Carlo Trombino, the store's manager, told him that the assistant manager, Suzanne Duffen, was leaving. Mr. Trombino offered Malcolm the job. He was pleased with Malcolm's work and his good horizontal and vertical relationships. Also, the assistant manager would have the opportunity to move up to store manager when Mr. Trombino opened his branch store.

Malcolm was stunned. He stammered a reply, "Could I think about it?" and left the office. All that day, Malcolm could not keep his mind on work. He kept wondering what he should do. Suzanne talked to him about it. She told him that she hoped he would accept the job. He had a lot of potential, and his future with Mr. Trombino looked good. His responsibilities on the job would increase, and he would have to work longer hours, but he would receive a nice raise and more benefits. At home that night, Malcolm was not even in the door when Ricardo, his roommate, told him that he was being transferred within the month. Malcolm would need to find a new roommate. Malcolm did not go to basketball practice that night—he had too much thinking to do. In 24 hours, his life had been turned upside down.

Case Study Analysis

a. What is the real problem?_____

_____

_____

b. What are the important facts to consider in this problem?_____

_____

_____

_____

c. What solutions to this problem can you think of? Describe a few. _____

_____

_____

_____

d. What would happen if the solutions you suggested were followed? Explain the results of each solution you described._____

_____

_____

_____

e. Of the solutions you described, which would you recommend? Why? _____

_____

_____

_____

Personal Assessment

What are the major sources of stress in your life? Use three sheets of paper, one for each stress area. Write a one-sentence description of the problem. Be specific. You have just completed Step 1 of the problem-solving process: Identify the problem. Now, do Step 2: Think of different solutions. On the appropriate sheet of paper, list all possible solutions. Do not censor yourself—include unrealistic solutions as well. Even a silly answer may have a kernel of truth in it. Now, complete Step 3: Decide which solution is best for you. Put your papers away for a week while you put your solution into action. After one week, do Step 4: Review your solution and adjust it if necessary.

Answers to Check Your Understanding: a. external, b.external, c. internal, d. external, e. external, f. internal, g. internal, h. external, i. external.

Chapter 14

HUMAN RELATIONS AND LEADERSHIP

After completing this chapter, you will be able to:

➤ *Distinguish between the human relations traits of good and poor leaders.*

➤ *Identify the leadership traits of people you know.*

Not everyone will become a president of a company, a general manager, or even a supervisor. Some people do not want to be leaders. In some careers, managing or leading other people is not a factor. And, of course, if everyone were a leader, who would follow?

You are just beginning a career and the possibility of leadership seems a long way off. However, this is the time to start developing leadership skills. If you do step into a managerial position someday, you cannot expect to learn leadership skills overnight. And when you need the skills is not the time to be learning them. Those who become managers get their skills as they go along. They improve their skills after becoming managers. So now, when you are starting out on your career, is a good time to begin learning what leadership involves.

Leadership Skills Help Everyone

There are many good reasons for thinking about leadership skills at this point. Even though everyone will not all become leaders, many people will need leadership skills outside their careers. You may be asked to take over the leadership of a fund-raising committee for a club or for your church or synagogue. You may lead a scouting troop, coach a Little League team, or serve as chairperson on the local school board. All people find themselves in a leadership position at some point in their life. Human relationships demand it from time to time.

Knowing leadership skills at this point can also help you to be a better worker. By knowing the skills, you will under-stand better what your supervisor is trying to do. You will learn by watching the strengths and weaknesses of other leaders, and you may even offer helpful advice to your own supervisor. Leadership skills, then, are really only human relations skills used in a specific way.

Leading vs. Bossing

You may think that being a supervisor is easy. Who needs human relations skills for that? Supervisors, after all, have the power of their position. People do what they are told or they get fired. Anybody can give orders.

Well, it may seem that way. But that is not what it is like. Sure, some managers get by just by ordering people about: "Do this ... Do that ... Don't do the other thing . . . ." Actually, this kind of person does not last long as a supervisor and is not likely to be productive.

Bossing people around is not leading them. You can get only so far trying to boss people. Ask yourself whether you like being bossed around. Not much, probably, unless you let the child aspect of character rule your life. In that case, you might like having a strong, bossy parent type around. But probably, like most people, you would rather be led than bossed.

Leaders get more out of people than bosses do. Consider Max and Cathy in the next example. Which one would you make your best effort for?

"Hey you," Max shouted. "Finish that report this afternoon!"

"I'm working on one report, and the department needs another one this

afternoon," Cathy said. "Could you try to get this one done? If you need any help, let me know, and I'll see what I can do."

Well, you might finish the report for Max. But you probably would resent his attitude and be inclined to do just an average job. You would not feel like doing anything extra for Max. With Cathy, though, you would be more willing to help. Her attitude would encourage you to join her effort to get all the work out.

Leadership Approaches

Several years ago, a psychologist named Douglas McGregor studied how businesses were run. He identified two basic ways in which management related to workers. He called these two different approaches to managing people Theory X and Theory Y. Perhaps after reading about them, you will find some more revealing names for these theories.

Theory X

Theory X is the traditional management approach. Management, McGregor said, had based its approach to workers on this philosophy for many years. Writing in the 1950s, McGregor said that Theory X was based upon the following assumptions:

- The average person does not like work and will avoid it whenever possible.

- Because people dislike work, they must be forced to do the work necessary to achieve the company's goals. Thus, people must be con-

trolled closely, directed completely, and threatened with punishment for failure to produce.

- The average person likes to be directed, wants to avoid responsibility, lacks ambition, and seeks security above all else.

What do you think of the Theory X approach to management? What would conditions be like in a place that manages people on the basis of these assumptions? Would you like to work in such a place? Do you think the assumptions are true for you? For others? Does the average person dislike work?

McGregor suggested that the assumptions of Theory X management were not based upon careful scientific study of human behavior. A few people, way back when industry was beginning its growth, may have said to each other, "Most of the other people are lazy. We'll have to force them to work in our factories." Or maybe they themselves did not like work and assumed that no one else did either. Or maybe the work was so demanding and unpleasant that no one did like it.

Work conditions were certainly different then. After all, not so very long ago workers were expected to work 12 hours a day, 6 days a week. They had no benefits as people today know them, and there was not much concern for workers' safety, comfort, or happiness.

Anyway, the Theory X assumptions were never closely examined, and over the years, the myth developed that people had to be forced to work. Some people let their parent self take charge, and they felt they had to order everyone else around.

As you can imagine, places that do operate today on Theory X assumptions are not the most pleasant places to work. They use the stick-force to prod workers along. Sometimes there is a carrot on the end of the stick—a pay raise. But mostly, in companies operating on Theory X assumptions, there is the stick: strict rules, close supervision, quick penalties, little freedom, and no real responsibility.

Theory Y

Today many companies try to base their approach to managing workers on what McGregor called *Theory Y* principles. According to McGregor, Theory Y is based on a realistic view of how people behave and why they do what they do. Theory Y takes into account that motivation must come from within and that workers who have objectives and goals will have the motivation to work. Theory Y is based on the following principles:

- Work is as natural for people as play or rest.

- People will work to achieve an objective to which they are committed without external controls or threats of punishment; people feel that reaching a goal to which they are committed is a reward in itself.

- The average worker, under proper conditions, will not only accept but also seek responsibility.

- Most people have the ability to use their imagination and creativity to solve company problems.

- Most modern jobs do not seriously challenge the ability of the average worker.

What do you think of management based on Theory Y assumptions? What would conditions be like in a company that manages people on the basis of Theory Y assumptions? Would you like to work in such a place? Do you think the assumptions are true for you? For other people? Do you think most people will work for goals they set themselves?

Although most companies today follow management procedures based on Theory Y assumptions, they generally concentrate on the first four. The last two assumptions are difficult to act on, especially in large companies employing hundreds of people. In addition, the last assumption deals with a characteristic of jobs that cannot easily be changed.

Management knows that some jobs can be boring. This is especially true of jobs on assembly lines. Many assembly-line production procedures were developed during World War II, when there was a shortage of trained workers. Managers broke jobs down into a lot of simple steps so that new workers could learn quickly and join the assembly line with little or no training. Workers could be replaced easily if they were called off to join the war effort or if they left for other reasons.

During the war, goods were needed badly, and production was the main concern. Today there has been a trend in the other direction, toward making jobs somewhat more complex and demanding. Instead of just standing and turning one or two screws all day, workers are given the chance to complete a whole unit by themselves. The intent, of course, is to motivate workers by stimulating their interest.

Leaders Need Human Relations Skills

You may think that the main qualifications for a leader are technical skills, a grasp of one's field, and superior knowledge. All of these are essential qualifications, but without basic human relations skills, a qualified person could still fail.

The best leaders are those who combine the ability to motivate people with technical skills or knowledge of their field. In fact, some people with inferior technical skills have made it as leaders on the strength of their human relations skills.

They surround themselves with people who have more technical expertise than they do, and they mold these experts into a team of willing workers.

At one time, it was believed that good leaders were born, not made. Leadership potential was thought to be inherited. Experience today shows that this is not the case.

Almost anyone can become an effective leader. Good leaders have developed their human relations skills for getting along with others. Those skills are the same ones that you have to know and use.

Leaders, of course, have a somewhat special point of view. Their basic aim is to get other people to do things. To be successful, they must develop the following human relations traits.

- Leaders do not let their feelings control them. When they are angry or annoyed, they do not explode. If they are frustrated, they do not sulk.

- Leaders tend to be more democratic than dictatorial. That is, they encourage those around them to participate in setting goals, assuming responsibility, and making decisions. They do not order people around.

- Leaders set realistic goals. This grows out of the democratic trait above. If more people are involved in setting goals, the goals are more likely to be realistic. Generally, a realistic goal is challenging but not impossible to achieve. Good leaders know that.

- Leaders are able to build group loyalty by seeing that workers are rewarded for their good work, both in deeds and in words. Effective leaders do not try to take all the credit for a job well done.

- Leaders are able to examine themselves and correct mistakes in their methods or their thinking.

- Leaders continually question themselves. They do not accept that everything they do is wonderful or right. They have the ability to examine their motives, their behavior, and performance. And they are able to accept constructive criticism and use it to improve their leadership abilities.

- Leaders are competitive. They want to win. The desire to excel, to be the best, is a motivation for them. They know that competition often pushes people to do just a little bit better job than if there were no competition. Leaders use this competitive urge to reach their own goals and their company's goals.

As you can see, all these traits are designed to make people feel important, needed and respected. Being able to do that is the essence of good human relations at any level.

Name _____   Date _____

Check Your Understanding

A good way to develop your leadership skills is to observe leaders around you. What makes you willing or unwilling to follow them?

1. The situations below describe several leaders. Ask yourself whether you would like to work under them. In the columns on the right, place a check mark to indicate whether they are good leaders or poor ones. After you have completed this exercise, compare your answers with those in the answer key on the last page of this chapter.

		Good Leader	Poor Leader
a.	Cindy decided that the workers under her were not producing enough. She felt they needed some goals so she spent a few evenings writing some for everyone under her. When she was finished, she handed the goals to the workers and told them they had better meet them.		
b.	All the workers knew exactly where they stood with Carmen, the plant manager. She did not like fooling around on the job, and she was hard on people who made careless errors. But she was ready to help when needed, and she always let everyone know exactly what was expected of them. When she had to make decisions concerning the workers, she asked them to participate and help her.		
c.	Colin was always driving the people under him at the photo developing plant. He was quick to punish them with fines and payless days off when they did not perform as he expected. This made Nate uncomfortable. He talked to Colin about his style of leadership, but Colin said, "That's the way I've always done it. I assume it ought to be done that way. Do you want to be let go?"		
d.	No one had to bother thinking in Sabina's department. She did it all for them. There was a certain way to do things and no one was allowed to do them any differently. When problems came up Sabina expected the workers to bring them to her. She felt that she was making life easy for the workers under her by having a rigid routine and eliminating their need to think as much as possible.		

2. In the space below, write out the reason for each of the evaluations you made above. How could those with poor leadership skills improve?

a. _____

_____

b. _____

_____

c. _____

_____

d. _____

_____

Case Study

In the situation below, there is a human relations problem. Read about it and then answer the questions to solve the problem. Write your answers in the space provided.

Brad was chosen for a management training program at the bank. As part of the training, he spent a month as temporary manager of a small branch of the bank. A supervisor observed and evaluated his performance.

Brad was determined to do well and show everyone he was a leader. He made sure he knew all the rules and regulations. He even added a few of his own. He decided, for one thing, that women could not wear pants suits. When they asked his reason, he said he just felt that women's pants suits did not fit the bank's image.

He was at work early every morning. He made it a point to check everyone in. If anyone was even a few minutes late, Brad would criticize that person in front of the whole staff. He knew that this was embarrassing, but he felt it served as a good warning to the others.

Some of the tellers in the branch were older employees who had been there for many years. To prove he was boss and not afraid of them, Brad made these senior employees change the way they did several things.

"You do it like this because I say so," he replied when some of the tellers tried to question him about the reason for the changes.

To demonstrate that he was alert and on top of things, Brad kept an eye on the tellers and watched what they did. If he did not like something, he did not hesitate to say so and correct the teller, even if a customer was there.

Brad felt that he had to assert himself and let everyone know who was running things. When the training program ended, he was surprised that he was not promoted to permanent manager.

Case Study Analysis

a. What is the real problem?_____

_____

_____

b. What are the important facts to consider in this problem?_____

_____

_____

_____

c. What solutions to this problem can you think of? Describe a few. _____

_____

_____

_____

_____

Name _____   Date _____

d. What would happen if the solutions you suggested were followed? Explain the results of each solution you described. _____

_____

_____

_____

_____

e. Of the solutions you described, which would you recommend? Why? _____

_____

_____

_____

_____

Personal Assessment

It is never too early to develop leadership skills. The first thing to do is to identify the skills that leaders around you have. Evaluate some people you know who have positions of authority. Do you think they are good leaders or just bosses?

Think of four leaders you know. Call them Leader A, Leader B, and so on. You may include teachers if you wish. In the space given below, list the characteristics of each leader. At the end of each list, give your evaluation—that is, state whether the person is a good leader or a poor one. Then, list your characteristics as a leader. Evaluate them as objectively as you can. Look at these lists and make a list of the general characteristics of a leader.

Leader A:_____

_____

_____

_____

Evaluation: _____

Leader B:_____

_____

_____

_____

Evaluation: _____

Leader C:_____

_____

_____

_____

_____

Evaluation: _____

Leader D:_____

_____

_____

_____

_____

Evaluation: _____

You:_____

_____

_____

_____

_____

Evaluation: _____

Make a list of the five most positive traits of a good leader._____

_____

_____

_____

_____

Make a list of the five most negative traits of a poor leader._____

_____

_____

_____

_____

Answers to Check Your Understanding: 1. a. Poor; b. Good; c. Poor; d. Poor.

Unit 3 Performance Mastery

Name _____ Date _____

A Working Vocabulary

Briefly define or identify each of the following terms. In the space provided, write your definitions or identifications using your own words. [Numbers refer to chapters where terms are introduced or discussed.]

Attitude [10, 12, 15, 17] _____

_____

Avoidance [13] _____

_____

Burnout [13] _____

_____

Denial [13] _____

_____

Horizontal relationship [12] _____

_____

Job satisfaction [12] _____

_____

Morale [12, 13] _____

_____

Motivation [9, 11, 12] _____

_____

Self-fulfilling prophecy [10] _____

_____

Stress [11, 13] _____

_____

Theory X [14] _____

_____

Theory Y [14] _____

_____

Vertical relationship [12] _____

_____

Discussion

In the space provided, write your answers to these questions using your own words.

a. What are six categories of requirements for a job? _____

_____

_____

b. What basic factors contribute to a person's motivation? _____

_____

_____

c. Why is motivation important? _____

_____

_____

d. What are the two basic sources of morale and job satisfaction? _____

_____

_____

e. Is it possible for a person to like a job and feel strong motivation but still have low morale? Explain._____

_____

_____

_____

f. Why is it important to have a positive attitude? _____

_____

_____

g. What are two important things to know about your attitude and its effect on you and your surroundings?_____

_____

_____

h. How can stress be both helpful and harmful? _____

_____

_____

i. Explain the difference between Theory X and Theory Y assumptions of managers. _____

_____

_____

_____

j. What are some traits that a good leader displays? _____

_____

_____

_____

Name _____   Date _____

Performance Assessment One

Your goal in this assessment is to evaluate yourself and determine whether you display a positive attitude or a negative attitude so that you may correct characteristics that suggest a negative attitude.

Place check marks in the rating table below to evaluate your behavior. Be as honest as possible. Do not be overly critical or too praiseworthy. When you have rated yourself, in the space provided below, list all the traits that you think are poor. Overall, is your attitude positive or negative? Brainstorm two or three concrete steps you can take to change each negative trait. Write those steps in the space below. Then try to change negative traits, working on the easiest ones first.

Trait	Very Good	Average	Poor
Posture			
Facial expression			
Interest in others			
Enthusiasm			
Respect for others			
Emotional control			
Initiative			
Dependability			
Self-confidence			
Loyalty			
Cheerfulness			
Ability to decide			
Ability to accept criticism			

Traits to Work On _____

_____

_____

Steps to Take_____

_____

_____

_____

_____

Performance Assessment Two

Your goal in this assessment is to see how attitude can either improve or harm human relations.

With your classmates, role-play the three situations below. Those who play the roles can decide what attitudes to reflect and then act them out. Those who observe the role playing will evaluate, in the space provided below, whether the two individuals showed positive or negative attitudes and whether their human relations skills helped to solve the problem. Use the following questions to evaluate each situation: What attitudes did the different people display? Could the situation have been handled better? In what way could either one have acted differently? Was the problem solved? Were the human relations good or poor? The situations are given below.

   a. A new, young supervisor must tell an employee who has been with the firm a long time that her or his work has been dropping below standard lately.
   b. Two workers are together in a rather small office. One likes to smoke and the other is bothered by smoke.
   c. A typist in an office pool feels he or she is doing most of the difficult work and has decided to talk to the office manager about it.

_____

_____

_____

_____

_____

_____

_____

_____

_____

_____

_____

_____

_____

UNIT 4

WORKING IN A MIXED SOCIETY

After completing this unit, you will be able to:

> ➤ *Demonstrate an awareness of the many different groups that make up this country.*

> ➤ *Recognize biases and stereotypes that hurt human relations.*

> ➤ *Use a positive approach to working with members of different groups.*

> ➤ *Use skills for dealing with biases and stereotypes.*

You live in a pluralistic society. What does it mean? Well, the root word is "plural"—more than one. A *pluralistic society* is a society in which many different ethnic, religious, racial, and cultural groups live side by side.

As a citizen of the United States, you are participating in the greatest ongoing social experiment ever tried. Part of the experiment—a large part—is to see whether people can govern themselves. This is a democracy.

Another part of the experiment is to open the country to everyone. The result has been that people from all over the world came here over the years. Some came long ago, others more recently. Perhaps your parents or your grandparents came to the United States.

That people came—not *when* they came—is the important thing. Few, if any, other countries have such a mix of people of different backgrounds, different races, and different religions.

Most people who came here did so of their own free will. Some left countries they no longer liked. Others were looking for a chance to make their fortunes. Others came so that they could practice their religion freely.

But some of the first people to come were kidnapped in Africa and brought

157

here by force. Given the chance, they might have come on their own. However, they were not given that chance. They were brought as slaves.

In time, African-Americans won their freedom, but they still suffered from racial discrimination. Even more than 100 years after slavery was declared illegal, many white people refused to admit African-American people into schools, jobs, and communities. Eventually, the federal government passed laws forbidding discrimination.

With the exception of one group, the different people who make up the United States today share the experience of having come here from someplace else. That one exception, of course, is the Native Americans, whom Columbus mistakenly called Indians. Native Americans were here already. This is their native land. Most Native Americans were killed by those invading their land. Their descendents are only now beginning to enjoy the civil rights that others take for granted.

For a long time, this country was called a melting pot. Americans were proud of that label. People from throughout the world came here, according to the melting pot idea, and mixed into the society so that everyone became alike.

But many people who came here did not want to drop everything that made them different. Africans, Vietnamese, Hispanics, and Chinese, among others, come from highly developed and original cultural backgrounds. They did not want to blend into a faceless whole. The idea began to grow, slowly, that there really was no need for everyone to fit into the same mold. Differences are good. They make the country more interesting.

It also was recognized, slowly, that there is no single best way for everyone to act, to be, or to look. So the melting pot has become more of a tossed salad. People are all mixed in here together, but they are all keeping their separate identities.

Having so many groups of people believing in different things, doing things in different ways, and looking different has created some confusion and problems. A weakness that most people share is a tendency to fear that which is different from them in any way. Of course, like all fears, this one goes away when people get to know and understand the differences. Sometimes, unfortunately, people do not take the time to understand.

It is no surprise that there are problems in this experiment. When many different kinds of people try to get along together, problems are bound to result. Think of your own family. You are all basically the same, right? But even the best of families have misunderstandings, arguments, fights and other problems. If, within your own family, you have to make an effort to get along, think of how much effort is needed in a society that includes all kinds of people.

What does all of this have to do with you and your career? Everything. As you pursue your career, you will be dealing with many of the different kinds of people who make up this country. How well you can do this will determine how successful you are in the long run. In this unit, you will read about the many groups that make up this society and the special problems they have met. And you will learn about some of the laws and human relations skills that help people to work successfully in this pluralistic society.

Chapter 15

ONE SOCIETY, MANY GROUPS

After completing this chapter, you will be able to:

➤ *Recognize that we all belong to many different groups.*

➤ *Identify four different discriminatory practices.*

➤ *Recognize harm caused by discrimination in the work place.*

➤ *Identify the groups that make up your community.*

During your working life, you are likely to meet and have to deal with many people who belong to groups different from the ones to which you belong. Yes, a person can belong to more than one group at a time. Everyone does, in fact.

You Belong to Many Groups

To begin with, you belong to one of the two major groups into which human beings fall: female and male. In addition, you are a member of some racial and *ethnic* group— that is, people who share a specific culture or language, such as Italian, Spanish, Irish, and so on.

You also have a sexual orientation. You may be mentally or physically disabled. You might belong to a religious group, a social group, a professional group, or a group that engages in a certain sport or hobby. You also belong to your personal family group.

Where you live has something to do with the groups with which you are associated. Northerners, Southerners, Midwesterners, mountain people, coastal people, city dwellers, country people—people in each of these groups have some things in common. They share things that set them apart from people in other groups.

Your socioeconomic status—how much money you have—is one of the most powerful groups you belong to.

You are also in a particular age group. And you can be grouped according to your physical characteristics. You may be tall, short, stocky, or skinny. Perhaps you are left-handed. If so, you are a member of a special *minority*, and you are reminded of it every time you use such a simple tool as ordinary scissors.

During your life, you will move from one group to another. You grow older. You may lose or gain weight. Your hair may fall out. You may become richer or poorer. You may become disabled. The important thing to remember, however, is that although you are part of several groups, you still are, and always will be, a unique individual.

It is easy enough to remember that about yourself. You know very well that you are an individual. You know exactly how you are like others in the groups you belong to, and you know how you differ from them. You probably are especially conscious of how you differ. You may get annoyed when an adult pegs you as "one of those teenagers." In the same way, a middle-aged person dislikes it when a young person says, "You can't trust anyone over thirty."

Relationships Among Groups

Groups are good things to have. It feels nice to belong to one. Everyone likes to have a sense of belonging, and being part of a special group gives people that feeling. But there is a danger here. Because people like the feeling of belonging to a special group, they begin to think their group is better, if not the best. Other groups, they decide, are not as good. They begin to think that groups that are different must somehow be bad or inferior. This feeling is strengthened by a natural fear of what is different.

Different? Yes. Bad? Inferior? Something to fear? No. Communication and human relations are destroyed when one group of people treats another group as bad. The poor treatment of one group by another group is called *discrimination*. Discrimination becomes particularly bad when one group has more members or controls the power in a community. Such a group (the *majority*) often uses its power to hurt the smaller or the less powerful group (the minority). The majority may voice a lot of reasons for discriminating against the minority. But such actions really are based on a fear of what is different and a desire to keep the minority from getting any power.

Minority Groups

The government identifies four minority groups: African-Americans, Spanish-speaking people, Native Americans, and Asian-Americans. In general, these people have suffered more from discrimination than any of the other groups that make up this country.

Besides these minority groups, the law recognizes several groups as deserving or requiring some form of protection against discrimination. These groups are called *protected classes*, and they include people of color, ethnic groups, women, old people, and religious groups. Also included are *disabled* people, those who have physical or mental handicaps.

Discrimination in the Work Place

In the world of work, discrimination has had particularly bad results. People who belong to minority groups have found it difficult to get good jobs and satisfying careers because the majority wanted to keep the best jobs for themselves.

Today it is against the law to practice this form of discrimination in the United States. As you read earlier, this country is an experiment. An experiment involves making mistakes and correcting them. The law now says that you cannot be denied a job because of your race, color, creed, sex, or handicap.

Some people have become discouraged with this country's experiment. They have grown up in poverty because their parents could not find jobs. The laws against discrimination cannot change the past, but they can change the future. You may find that discrimination still exists in the job market. That is not surprising. Discrimination is tough to wipe out. It is not an American invention. The sad truth is that discrimination exists throughout the world. But these new laws are an attempt to correct the situation here.

Some people—those who are in the majority—may fear these laws believing that it gives minority groups an unfair edge in the job market. But these laws are intended only to eliminate the unfair edge that the majority has enjoyed in the past. They provide for honest competition in the job market. People with the right skills and attitude need never fear honest competition.

In the long run, the laws against discrimination in employment protect all workers. As long as there is discrimination, there will be a pool of cheap labor. That is because employers are able to offer jobs at low pay to those unable to find good-paying jobs because of discrimination. Having a pool of cheap labor helps employers keep all wages down. Illegal aliens get the lowest pay, way below minimum wage.

Forms of Job Discrimination

You can see that job discrimination is a large human relations problem from the number of complaints that have been filed with the Equal Employment Opportunity Commission (EEOC). The EEOC is a federal commission charged by law to investigate and correct discriminatory practices found in companies with more than 15 employees. Not all cases of discrimination are reported to the EEOC, and not all businesses are under its jurisdiction. Yet one report showed that 107,846 charges were filed with the EEOC in a single year.

A breakdown of these charges showed that nearly 54,000 were made because of racial discrimination. There were nearly 34,000 charges of discrimination because of sex. More than 12,000 charges concerned discrimination because of a person's national origin (ethnic group). And there were 2,200 charges of religious discrimination. The other charges were made for miscellaneous reasons.

How are minority groups discriminated against? An early EEOC report said that race discrimination usually took the following forms: being let go, terms and conditions of employment, hiring and promotion, wages, and retaliation—in that order of frequency. People of minority groups had to have more qualifications and do more to be hired or promoted. They were hired last and fired first. And they were paid less for the same work.

Discrimination based on sex usually took the following forms, in order of frequency: wages, terms and conditions of employment, discharge (being let go), promotion, hiring, and job classification. Women were paid less for doing the same work as men. They were denied jobs and promotions because of their sex.

In addition to federal laws, several states have their own laws prohibiting discrimination.

Identifying Discriminatory Practices

Because there are laws against discriminatory practices, officials upholding the laws, together with the courts, have had to establish some guidelines for defining discrimination. It is worth knowing what some of these guidelines are. Knowing them may help you in filing a complaint if you are a victim. And knowing these standards can help all people improve human relations.

Many people act in a discriminatory way toward others simply because they do not stop to think. They have been raised to believe certain things or think in certain ways. These beliefs are found in their parent selves. When they let their parent self control their relations with other groups, they are likely to create human relations problems.

By thinking about the standards given below and applying them to your personal situations, you can avoid some human relations problems. The standards were set up to guide companies in dealing with employees.

Differential Treatment

If you treat someone in a different way from everyone else just because that person is from another group, then you are practicing discrimination.

An example of this type of discrimination would be a company that keeps four inefficient, ineffective workers while firing a disabled person whose job record is no worse.

Some company rules have had unintentional discriminatory effects because not all potential employees have had the same advantages. Such rules, in effect, give majority workers the advantage.

In one such incident, the courts ruled that a high school diploma could not be required of all job applicants because this had the effect of screening out minority applicants.

In this particular state, fewer minority applicants had the chance to finish high school.

Also, at one time, this company had not required workers to have a high school diploma, and workers who were hired without one were able to do the job just as well as those who had a diploma.

The company had added the requirement in order to keep minority members out, and so the requirement was ruled discriminatory.

Indirect Discrimination

Sometimes discrimination is practiced in indirect ways. Here is one example:

An African-American manager was fired because she performed less well after being demoted. An investigation showed that the manager had been demoted for racial reasons.

Since her work became poor because of the demotion, and since the demotion was discriminatory, firing her for poor work was found to be—at least in part—discriminatory too.

To put people into lower positions because of the groups they belong to and then to blame them for their behavior in response to this action is a particularly harsh form of discrimination.

Blaming Minority Groups for Problems

It is considered discrimination if a company fires a minority-group member on the grounds that he or she cannot get along with the majority group. This most often happens in cases of race discrimination, but it also occurs because of sex, age, or handicaps.

It puts minority members in a trap. First, they are treated differently because they belong to a minority group. Then, they are blamed because they "need" special treatment. Such circular reasoning is damaging to everyone.

Forced Action

It is also considered discriminatory when a worker feels forced into taking an action that is not in his or her best interest because of conditions created by co-workers prejudiced against the minority individual.

For example, if other workers constantly insult you because of your sex, age, religion, or ethnic group, you may get angry enough to quit.

When this happens, the courts have found that the company was guilty of discriminatory discharge because it allowed the work atmosphere to become difficult and painful for the minority-group member.

Companies Responsible

Even though the worker actually resigned from the job, the company was found to be at fault for allowing discrimination to create such a bad situation that it forced an individual to take an action not in his or her own best interest.

The ruling implies that companies can not simply ignore the atmosphere generated in their work areas, particularly when their employees act in discriminatory ways toward co-workers.

Name _____   Date _____

Check Your Understanding

A good way to learn whether or not you discriminate unfairly is to see how you feel about that practice on the job. Certain types of behavior have been identified as standards for determining whether a company has been guilty of discriminatory practices. Read each statement below. Then select the phrase on the left that best describes what took place. Write the phrase number in the answer space provided at the right. You may use a phrase more than once . After you have completed the exercise, compare your answers with those in the answer key on the last page of this chapter.

1. Differential treatment	a.	The All-Routes Travel Agency had a policy that all agents must be six feet tall and weigh at least 180 pounds. Mona, who wanted to be a travel agent, was turned down because she was not tall enough. She filed a charge of discrimination on the grounds that most women are under six feet.	a.___
2. Indirect discrimination	b.	Callie was the only African-American cook at the Cozy Cupboard Restaurant. She was also the only one who was asked to wash the floors and clean out the restrooms. She filed a charge of discrimination.	b.___
3. Blaming minority groups f or problems	c.	Yeun passed up the chance to become a supervisor because several workers let him know they would not like to work under someone of his race. Later he decided he would like to try it anyway, but the company said no because he had passed up his chance. Yeun claimed he was denied a promotion because of discrimination.	c.___
4. Forced action	d.	Imelda was upset when one or two other workers made remarks about her racial background. She could not put it out of her mind. As a result, her work began to suffer. She was not as quick, and she made many mistakes. Finally, she was fired. Imelda sued to get her job back. She claimed that her work suffered because of the racial remarks and that, therefore, the real reason for her discharge was discrimination, not poor work.	d.___
	e.	Susan was the only woman on the oil exploration crew. She did her work well—better than several others. But the company fired her. They said that men could not get used to having a woman on the crew. Susan sued for her job and charged the company with discrimination.	e.___

Case Study

In the situation given below, there is a problem. Read the situation and then answer the questions to solve the problem. Write your answers in the space provided.

"Mr. Mann, I think I'm going to quit and look for another job."

"What? Why do you want to do that? You are one of our best new machinists, Brian. I thought you liked it here."

"Well, I do mostly, but some things bother me."

"Don't you like the work? I thought you wanted to be a machinist. The pay is good, and your chances of promotion are very good."

"Oh, I like the work all right. And I do want to be a machinist. But I want to find a place where I'll be more comfortable."

"What do you mean?"

"Well, I don't feel comfortable. I mean, you know, there are all sorts of people working here. There are even women machinists."

"So what?" Mr. Mann said. "We hire people no matter what their sex, race, or ethnic background is. Sure, we have all kinds of people. I mean, that's how this country is.

"Not the small town I come from," Brian said. "People who are different from me make me feel, like I said, uncomfortable. It's not just the women, although I never worked with them before. But many workers here have different backgrounds from mine. I'd rather work with my own kind of people. I'm going to quit."

"Where will you find another job?"

"I don't know. I'll look around," Brian said.

Case Study Analysis

a. What is the real problem?_____

_____

_____

b. What are the important facts to consider in this problem?_____

_____

_____

c. What solutions to this problem can you think of? Describe a few. _____

_____

_____

_____

d. What would happen if the solutions you suggested were followed? Explain the results of each solution you described._____

_____

_____

_____

Name _____   Date _____

e. Of the solutions you described, which would you recommend? Why? _____

_____

_____

_____

_____

Personal Assessment

To get an idea of what a great variety of people live in this country, look at your own community. Check at the library to see whether there are any publications of the U.S. Census Bureau that give statistics about the makeup of your community. Find out what groups are represented and what their size is. Check telephone directories to get a rough idea of all the different nationalities reflected by the family names. City directories can help also. You also can write to the U.S. Census Bureau in Washington, D.C., for information about your area. If other sources are unavailable, determine what your classmates' backgrounds are. You probably know many all ready. In the space below, write a report describing who goes into the tossed salad of your community. Share the results with your class.

_____

_____

_____

_____

_____

_____

_____

_____

_____

_____

_____

_____

_____

_____

_____

_____

_____

_____

_____

_____

_____

_____
_____
_____
_____
_____
_____
_____
_____
_____
_____
_____
_____
_____
_____
_____
_____
_____
_____
_____
_____
_____
_____
_____
_____
_____
_____
_____
_____
_____
_____
_____
_____
_____
_____
_____
_____
_____
_____

Answers to Check Your Understanding: a. Differential treatment; b. Differential treatment; c. Forced action; d. Indirect discrimination; e. Blaming minority groups for problems.

Chapter 16

LABELING OTHERS

After completing this chapter, you will be able to:

➤ *Identify problems caused by stereotypes, biases, and prejudices.*

➤ *Recognize the biases present in common generalizations.*

There is nothing more convenient than being able to put a label on a person. It makes life simple.

"Oh, there's so-and-so. She's a such-and-such."

So-and-so has been neatly labeled and put into a pigeonhole. Now you know all about her. You have stereotyped her.

Stereotypes

In Unit 2, you learned about generalizations and how dangerous they can be. A *stereotype* is a generalization in one of its most dangerous forms. Stereotypes do more to hinder human relations than any other form of generalization.

Here is how a stereotype works. People consider only one or two facts about an entire group of people and apply them to each individual. Often, in this country, this is done on the basis of sex or skin color. But it also happens because of family background, age, religion, sexual orientation, or handicaps.

People who use stereotypes consider all those who fit into any group as identical. One group member is just like every other member.

As you know, however, no two people are identical. So it is always unfair to apply stereotypes to individuals. Even flattering stereotypes are harmful, such as "African-Americans have good rhythm." "Asian-Americans are smart." They are harmful because they deny individuality to people who make up the group. They are harmful because they encourage others to expect individuals in a group all to behave in a certain way.

Biases and Prejudices

A bad thing about using a stereotype in thinking about people is that it will strengthen a bias you have. A *bias* is an unthinking opinion about something or somebody. Remember that people like the sense of belonging to one group and tend to fear different groups that they do not understand. Also, to make their group seem superior, they might try to put down all groups that are different. In this way, they develop biases.

A person with many strong biases is said to be *prejudiced*, which means pre-judging. Prejudiced people judge others without considering all the facts. They jump to conclusions without thinking at all.

Generalizations are Imperfect

A funny thing about groups is that although most people want to belong to them, they do not want to be judged only by the groups they belong to. Also, people are sometimes grouped or stereotyped in ways that they would rather not be. "She's a redhead. You know what tempers they have." In fact, this person might be sweet and calm. But that does not cross the mind of a person who has a stereotype of redheads. To that person, all redheads have bad tempers.

At one time, people thought that all left-handed people were evil. That was a tough stereotype to fight against. "Blondes have more fun." (A lot of hair dye has been sold to people who think in stereotypes.) "You can't trust a skinny person." "Fat people are more jolly." Ho hum.

As you read earlier, all generalizations are loose and imperfect. Stereotypes, too, are loose and imperfect. They simply are not true. Therefore, it is impossible to take one fact about a group of people and apply it to all the people in that group. Everyone is unique, and everyone wants to be considered an individual—to feel important. A thinking person will enjoy the differences among individuals.

Biases are Everywhere

Everyone has biases. You like some people. You dislike others. You may even dislike whole groups. But you should always wait to label people until after you have met them and seen them function. You may not like people who brag and talk loudly. Or you may not like practical jokers. Such likes are logical and not bad in themselves. They are bad when you apply them randomly.

Use your human relations skills to overcome. As you establish your values and self-identity, you will recognize biases that have been absorbed in your parent aspect. The following story shows how widespread unconscious biases may be:

A father and his son were in an automobile accident. The father was killed immediately. The son, critically injured, was rushed to a near-by hospital. The doctor entering the operating room, looked at the boy, and said, "I can't operate on him. He's my son."

People who were told this story were asked, "How can this be?" Most suggested that the father had not really been killed or that the man killed was the stepfather, whereas the doctor was the real fa-ther of the boy. Few people gave the right answer: "The doctor is the boy's mother."

The belief that certain jobs are for men only is an illustration of how deep some biases go. Even the many job names reflect this bias: foreman, chairman.

Some people hold stereotypes so firmly in the parent aspect that they must work hard to control their biases. If they are not careful, their biases come out automatically. When that happens, their human relations are damaged.

Women—who make up a large part of the work force—suffer from many forms of obvious and not-so-obvious discrimination. A male supervisor may reveal his bias by the different way he talks to a male worker and to a female worker. A biased supervisor talks with a male worker:

Calm down.

What's your work experience?

Would you like to move up to a higher position in the office?

You've been late a few times. Try to get here on time in the future.

A biased supervisor talks with a female worker:

Take it easy, sweetheart.

Are you married?

You wouldn't want to move up. You'd feel uncomfortable working with all men.

You'd better cut out the dates, Jane, if you can't get here on time.

Gender-Based Bias

Bias against women has developed over the centuries in most societies. It is so strong that women as well as men sometimes accept the stereotype that women are supposed to be the servants of men. As a result, everyone should examine biases against women carefully, since they are widespread and are accepted automatically.

Gender-based biases stereotype men as well. Many people think that only women can be nurses, kindergarten teachers or childcare providers. They think that men are not capable of nurturing. Other people stereotype men in certain occupations, such as hairdressers or ballet dancers.

Take that old saying, "A woman's place is in the home." This statement reflects a standard stereotype of women and a bias against their being any place else. Human relations problems enter in when the bias against women's being any place else crops up.

There is nothing wrong with being a homemaker. It is a good, honorable life for anyone, male or female. In fact, the argument could be made that raising children and keeping a family together is one of the most challenging, necessary, and interesting things a person can do. On the job market, the skills demanded for this work would be up in the top-management level, at least. But to suggest that women should be found nowhere but in the home is prejudiced and biased.

A person thinking of women in terms of a homemaker stereotype overlooks the obvious facts. Women are no longer only in the home. More than 54 million women work outside of their homes. They make up 44 percent of the work force—which is nearly half. Not only are large numbers of women working, but they work for the same reasons that men do: money, self-satisfaction, and fulfillment.

Dealing With Stereotypes

Denying that you have any biases or stereotypes is not the best way to handle them. Rather, become aware of them and do not let them get between you and the individuals you meet and to whom you must relate. To help you maintain good human relations when dealing with members of groups different from yours, remember the following basic guidelines:

- People like to be treated as individuals. They become offended when they are treated unfairly because they are part of a group.

- True stereotypes do not exist in the real world. Applying the general to the individual does not work, and hurts and confines the individual as well as those outside the group.

- Do not fear what is different. Get to know and to understand people who are different from you. Be tolerant, at least, of other people's differences and cultures. Try to learn to appreciate them.

- Always treat others with respect.

Name _____   Date _____

Check Your Understanding

Begin to detect your own biases by completing the following exercise. Read the following statements. Decide whether each is true or false and put a check mark in the appropriate column to the right. After you have completed the exercise, compare your answers with those in the answer key on the last page of this chapter.

		True	False
a.	A person who uses stereotypes thinks that every person in a given group is practically identical to every other person in the group.		
b.	Using stereotypes reflects your biases.		
c.	Although everyone likes to belong to a special group, people are sometimes labeled in ways they would rather not be.		
d.	Both men and women work for money and fulfillment.		
e.	Some stereotypes are flattering.		
f.	It is easy to hide our biases.		
g.	More than 54 million women work outside the home.		
h.	Almost half of the work force is made up of women.		
i.	The best way to handle your biases is to deny that you have them.		
j.	People like to be treated as individuals.		
k.	You need to fear that which is different.		

Case Study

In the situation below, there is a human relations problem. Read about it and then answer the questions to solve the problem. Write your answers in the space provided.

"Dumb blonde," Adam said with an angry shrug. "What do you expect?" "Come on," Bill said. "Anyone could have made that mistake." Bill and Adam worked as programmers in a large computer company. As senior programmers, they checked the work of the new workers. Adam was commenting on an error a new programmer had made.

Later, during a lunch break, Adam was talking with several other programmers. "Well, you really can't expect women to understand the mechanics of this," he said. He either did not see or ignored the angry stares from some of the women.

"I don't know about that," Shelley, who was an excellent programmer, said. "Some of us are very good at it."

"Good—for women, that is," Adam shot back.

In the afternoon, Adam yelled rudely at Mary for doing something that he thought was wrong. When she argued with him, he said, "just like a woman. Can't take criticism."

"I can take criticism when it is justified and when it is given right," Mary said. "But not only were you rude this time, you were wrong."

The head supervisor came over to find out what was wrong. When he inspected the work in dispute, he found that Mary had done it perfectly. Adam was mistaken when he corrected her. Adam walked away without apologizing. He just muttered something about women being hard to work with.

Case Study Analysis

a. What is the real problem?_____

_____

b. What are the important facts to consider in this problem?_____

_____

_____

_____

c. What solutions to this problem can you think of? Describe a few. _____

_____

_____

_____

d. What would happen if the solutions you suggested were followed? Explain the results of each solution you described._____

_____

_____

_____

e. Of the solutions you described, which would you recommend? Why? _____

_____

_____

_____

Personal Assessment

The world is full of phrases and statements that reflect biases or set up stereotypes—phrases such as "All English people like tea," or "All fat people are jolly." On a separate sheet of paper, list as many such meaningless phrases as you can. Check books, magazines, radio, newspapers, television, relatives, and friends. Include ones you may be using yourself, or that your family or friends use. Classify the statements as to sexism, racism, ageism, ethnic background, and other traits. For each classification, pick the statement that you think is most meaningless and read it to the class.

Answers to Check Your Understanding: a. T; b. T; c. T; d. T; e. T; f. F; g. T; h. T; i. F; j. T; k. F.

Chapter 17

BIAS IN THE WORK PLACE

After completing this chapter, you will be able to:

➤ *Recognize the necessity to relate to others.*

➤ *Identify biased and defensive reactions in human behavior.*

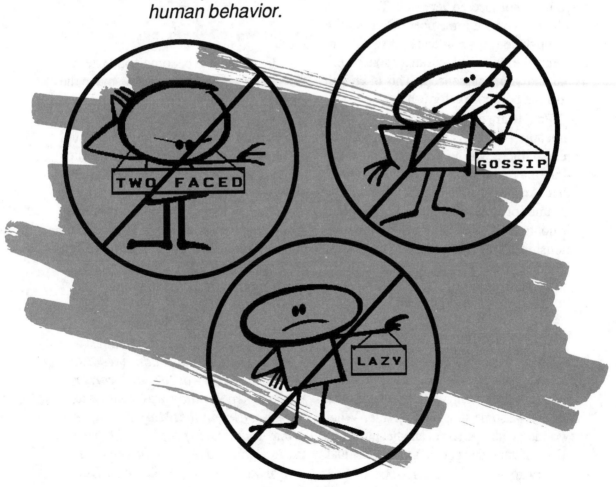

In almost any career you choose, you will have to work with other people. Two basic factors influence your relationships with them: your background (self-identity, values, and ethnic, racial, and religious groups) and the background of others. In some situations, you may belong to the minority group. In others, you may belong to the majority. In both cases, you operate within the framework of your background.

How you get along with others will affect your job performance. If you allow differences that exist among people to influence your relationships and judgments, you will not succeed very well. This is true whether you are a member of a minority group or not. Any bias that keeps you from seeing the individual will affect your potential and your self-concept. This often will result in poor job performance.

People are different. When they work in teams—which is essential in most careers—there will be tensions. The situation may never be perfect. Recognize that. Accept it. Bias is a fact that will be around for some time to come. The point is not to let it affect your on-the-job relationships. This is important to remember whether you are the victim of bias or the one who displays it.

Relate to Others as Individuals

You will be working with people of other groups at some time in your life. When working with a person of another group, try to understand that person as an individual.

Try to wipe all labels, good or bad, from your mind. Say to yourself, "Here

is another individual, a human being. This person has the same basic needs I have and probably has similar goals." Evaluate the person on the basis of your day-to-day experiences.

You may decide that the person has bad work habits or is annoying in other ways, and you may not want to become friends. That is all right if your decision is based on daily, fair evaluation and not on bias. By regarding the person as an individual and not a member of this or that group, the chances are that you will develop a good working relationship even if you never become close friends.

Prejudiced or Preferential Treatment

You do not have to become good friends. No one asks that. Some people make the mistake of thinking they must bend over backward to be nice to members of every other group. They think they should not see anything wrong or unpleasant in such individuals. That, of course, is silly. People who play this game are as guilty of prejudice as those who think minority-group members are all bad. They still are treating people of other groups differently, rather than treating everyone the same. Lindsay is a case in point:

Lindsay was an excellent supervisor at a factory that made videocassettes. Mark was a new worker under her. Lindsay was white and very conscious that Mark was black and that black people have been discriminated against. She was determined to be more than fair in this regard.

Lindsay went out of her way to welcome Mark and make him feel at ease. This was Mark's first job, and he was eager to learn. Because he was new, he had much to learn. But he began to find it difficult to learn. Whenever he slowed down or had a problem, Lindsay would hurry over and help. She would try to make things easier for him by doing some of the work herself. Or she would not ask him to do as much as she asked some other workers to do. She would correct Mark's mistakes without telling him what he should do differently.

Finally Mark had to speak to Lindsay. "Look," he. said, "I appreciate all the help and what you are doing for me, but you have got to let me make it on my own, just like any other worker. I don't want to be treated any differently."

That opened Lindsay's eyes. In trying to help Mark, she had treated him differently. After their talk, she reacted to Mark and his mistakes just as she did to everyone else. Soon he was one of the top producers. Then Lindsay could begin treating him differently again—as a top producer.

Lindsay was trying too hard to avoid any bias she may have had. As the story shows, that can be as unproductive as showing a negative bias. She was not giving Mark a fair chance to prove whether or not he was a good worker. If he had turned out to be a poor worker, she should not have given him special treatment because of his skin color any more than she should have held that against him.

Become Aware of Bias

An out-and-out display of prejudice is so obvious and so likely to trigger an immediate and unwanted response that most people are careful to control it. But the less obvious forms of bias can also destroy good relations on the job too. This is true whether the bias is displayed in a negative way or through well-meaning efforts to make allowances, as Lindsay did.

Many phrases that people use unthinkingly when they talk to minorities reflect bias and can be annoying to the receiver:

- "I thought all you people liked . . ."

- "How do you people feel about . . ."

- "Gee, you did a good job for a . . ."

- "That comes naturally for you . . ."

Ethnic or racial humor—jokes whose points revolve around supposed characteristics of a particular group—can be especially offensive. When people of different backgrounds get to know each other well, they may use this kind of humor on each other to show their trust and respect. But using such humor in general situations is unkind.

Women are particular victims of a continuing, unthinking bias on the part of men. Many men think that women like to be flirted with. These men think it is all right to call women pet names or address terms of endearment to them. The stereotype of women as weak and helpless, or scatterbrained and vain, is still around. Deirdre experienced this type of bias:

Deirdre and two other women worked in an office with several men. The men would playfully put their arms around the women. Sometimes the men called them "dear," even in business conversations. Naturally, all this annoyed the women.

"I'm sure most of them don't mean anything by this, although, with some, I'm not so sure," Deirdre said. "Anyway, I feel that there is no reason—at any time— for the men to put their hands on us. We don't encourage them. Perhaps we haven't properly discouraged them. But we did not feel it necessary to make a scene over such a supposedly innocent gesture as a touch on the shoulder or an arm around the waist." But the women were always faced with the problem of putting up with this innocent (but biased) gesture or being accused of making a scene over nothing.

"I hate to cause embarrassment," Deirdre said. *"But it makes me angry. These men would never treat other men that way. The only reason they do it is because we're women. They don't feel any real respect for us as co-workers and as their equals. The only way they feel they can deal with us is by teasing."*

Many women also do not get the respect all workers deserve from employers. Some bosses ask women to run errands that they would never expect from men, such as making coffee, buying gifts, and planning staff parties. In staff meetings, women are often expected to take the notes, but they are also likely to be left out of the final decision-making process.

Do Not Patronize Others

If you are a member of a minority group, you may feel especially angry when people *patronize* you—that is, treat you as a child and give you special handling. Everyone hates to be patronized; it is quite offensive.

In the example earlier, Lindsay was patronizing Mark by doing his work for him and not letting him learn from his mistakes. People with foreign accents are often patronized. Some well-meaning but uninformed people will talk with them in a loud voice or use simple expressions that are almost baby talk. Just because people speak with an accent is no reason to suppose they are hard of hearing or unintelligent. Rosa met up with this type of patronizing:

Rosa spoke with an Italian accent. When she began working on a new job, the supervisor talked slowly and loudly. Then the supervisor had a good idea. She called in Alfonso, who spoke Italian, to help explain things to Rosa. Rosa politely pointed out that she had spoken English since she was a girl and had a high school diploma. She did not need an interpreter, nor was she hard of hearing.

Glenn was the victim of another type of patronizing attitude, but he did not have an accent:

Glenn spoke English perfectly. He held a college degree. Both he and his parents were born in the United States. His grandparents came from Japan. Glenn was as American as a person can be—a second-generation American native. Yet, because he looked Asian, thoughtless people often said stupid things to him. A question he particularly hated was, "Gee, do you ever miss your country?" Glenn learned to reply, "I really couldn't say. I've never left it."

Avoiding the outright expression of bias is fairly easy. But you must also guard against patronizing attitudes that can destroy good public relations on the job.

Defensive Reactions

Perhaps the hardest thing to avoid if you are a member of a minority group is becoming defensive. *Defensive* people are always protecting themselves. They overreact. They act as though they really needed to defend themselves from an attack or criticism. Remember that any attack or criticism based on bias is unjustified. The first thing to do is to ignore it.

If a prejudiced person continues to be offensive or if you cannot ignore the problem, try to correct the person as calmly and as clearly as you can. Avoid reacting by insulting the prejudiced person. That may make you feel good for the

moment, but it will settle nothing in the long run. It will just add to the friction and lack of communication between you.

If you continue to suffer from prejudice on the job, talk with your supervisor about it. Try to state your case as unemotionally as possible. Ask for a good-faith effort to solve the problem. Look for a solution, not for revenge.

If the problem continues, notify your supervisor in writing. Again show your willingness to try to solve the problem. Putting the matter into writing will provide proof that you have made an honest, sincere effort to have the situation corrected. Then if the problem continues, file a formal grievance with your company. Most companies have grievance procedures for situations such as this.

If your company does not have formal grievance procedures or fails to solve the problem, you still have some choices open. You can quit your job and look for work elsewhere. Quitting your job should be your last resort. Also, you can try to live with the problem. You can seek advice and help from a local civil rights agency. Local civil rights organizations can help explain your rights and help you to protect them under the law. These organizations will be able to tell you what state and federal agencies can help.

Here is how filing a charge of discrimination with the EEOC works:

First you will be interviewed about your complaint to determine whether it is against the law. If the commission or agency thinks your case has merit, it will try to settle the case. You may be compensated for what you have lost: pay or a job.

If the case cannot be settled, court action may be necessary. Some state agencies will handle the case for you. In other states, or if the EEOC handles the case, you may have to get your own lawyer. A company cannot legally fire you or punish you for making a charge against it.

Being on the receiving end of biased remarks and actions is not easy. It takes skill at human relations to handle such situations and correct the problems. It is not fair, but members of minority groups sometimes have to work harder than others to maintain good human relations.

Discrimination Hurts

People whose physical characteristics put them into special groups experience obvious forms of discrimination. But people can discriminate against anyone who is different for any reason. People whose religious beliefs differ from the majority—such as the Amish, Jews, Quakers, and Muslims—have been victims of prejudice.

People who speak another language are often victims. Workers from Cuba, Mexico, or Puerto Rico who speak Spanish or English with an accent are sometimes discriminated against. Why the ability to speak two languages is not appreciated by biased people is one of the many mysteries surrounding bias.

That bias is unthinking can be seen in the experiences of people who suffered discrimination after coming to this country and then suffered discrimination when they returned to their original countries. That happened to Luisa:

When Luisa was young, her parents brought her to the United States from Puerto Rico. At first, she had difficulty in school because she only spoke Spanish. Other kids picked on her. They made fun of her and showed her she did not belong.

Luisa learned to speak English and adjusted to life here. But shortly after she graduated from high school, her parents moved back to Puerto Rico, taking Luisa with them. "Well," Luisa thought, "at least I will belong again."

Poor Luisa. In Puerto Rico, she found that many people considered her an outsider—someone from "the States." Some made fun of her accent, which had changed while she had lived in New York. Others made fun of how she dressed and did things. When she was in New York, many people made her feel she was an outsider because she was from Puerto Rico. Back in Puerto Rico, many people made her feel she was an outsider because she had lived in New York.

The truth, of course, is that Luisa was just an individual. She had her share of abilities and her share of failings. She would have preferred to have been judged on the basis of those.

Discrimination is unthinking. It hurts every one. Your best chance for success in any field is to forget stereotypes and deal with individuals.

Name _____   Date _____

Check Your Understanding

See whether you are aware of bias and defensive reactions in human relations. Read the situations described below. Decide whether the person is practicing good human relations or poor human relations. Then place a check mark in the appropriate column on the right. After you have completed the exercise, compare your answers with those in the answer key on the last page of this chapter.

		Good	Poor
a.	Bill had been selected to organize the company barbecue in the park. He had to estimate how many people would attend. "I guess Jerry won't go," he thought "because he is in a wheelchair and wouldn't enjoy it at all."		
b.	Frances treated the new worker from Puerto Rico just like everyone else. When someone suggested that he needed special attention because of his accent, Frances disagreed. She said that the new worker had to make it on his own and that it would be no favor to treat him any differently from other workers.		
c.	I interviewed a person today for the receptionist's position. She told me about her grandchildren. My boss would like me to hire a younger woman instead, but this person has a better attitude, so I want to offer her the job.		
d.	When Juanita, who was a Mexican American, began to work, the supervisor assigned her to work with another Mexican American because "she would feel more comfortable working with her own kind."		
e.	Despite the objections of several people, the superintendent ruled that female coaches must be paid the same amount of money that the male coaches were.		

Case Study

In the situation below, there is a human relations problem. Read about it and then answer the questions to solve the problem. Write your answers in the space provided.

Anselmo was a stock clerk in a large hardware store. He was intelligent, ambitious, and hard-working. He learned quickly, and soon he knew a great deal about the tools, supplies, and equipment that the store sold. Anselmo began to look forward to becoming a salesperson.

But when he asked Mr. Halloran, the store manager, for an opportunity to wait on customers, Mr. Halloran told him there were no openings. Mr. Halloran was very nice to Anselmo and told him he was doing a fine job as a stock clerk. He even gave him a small raise. Sometimes, when work was slow, Mr. Halloran would ask Anselmo questions about interesting places to see in Puerto Rico, where Anselmo used to live. (Mr. Halloran was thinking of going there on a cruise the next winter.)

Anselmo was surprised when two new sales clerks were hired to wait on customers in the store. "Why," he wondered to himself, "would Mr. Halloran tell me there are no openings and then hire two other people when he seems to like my work and even thinks I deserve a raise?"

He was trying to decide whether to ask Mr. Halloran again politely for a chance as a salesperson or to protest and demand an explanation, when he accidentally overheard Mr. Halloran talking to Sandy Brouwer, the assistant manager.

"Sure, Sandy, I know Anselmo's an excellent worker, and he really wants the chance to move up. I'd like to help him, but I've got to think of the effect on business. His Spanish accent is just too strong. I think he would turn customers away from us. You know, this community has a lot of prejudice against Puerto Ricans."

"But, Mr. Halloran," answered Sandy, "quite a few of our customers are Spanish-speaking themselves. Would they be turned away or feel more welcome? And Anselmo might be even more help in showing the rest of the community how foolish their prejudice is."

Anselmo had heard enough. Fighting to control his temper, he walked away to think about what he should do.

Case Study Analysis

a. What is the real problem?_____

_____

_____

b. What are the important facts to consider in this problem?_____

_____

_____

_____

c. What solutions to this problem can you think of? Describe a few. _____

_____

_____

_____

d. What would happen if the solutions you suggested were followed? Explain the results of each solution you described._____

_____

_____

_____

e. Of the solutions you described, which would you recommend? Why? _____

_____

_____

_____

_____

Name _____   *Date* _____

Personal Assessment

Bias in human relations is sometimes difficult to pin down. Minority-group members may be defensive, while the majority often are unaware of how they are discriminating. To make yourself more aware of discrimination, and to improve your own human relations, talk with some people from racial, ethnic, or religious backgrounds that are different from yours. Learn what their hopes and fears are, and what they want to do in life. Find out how you really differ and how you are alike. Discover each other as individuals as well as members of different groups.

Afterwards, write an essay on discrimination, in the space that follows, identifying yourself as a minority-group member or a majority-group member on the basis of sex , race, ethnic group, economic group, and age. Tell how belonging to one group or the other can affect your career plans. How does it affect your human relations? Does it affect people's basic human needs?

_____

_____

_____

_____

_____

_____

_____

_____

_____

_____

_____

_____

_____

_____

_____

_____

_____

_____

_____

_____

_____

_____

_____

_____
_____
_____
_____
_____
_____
_____
_____
_____
_____
_____
_____
_____
_____
_____
_____
_____
_____
_____
_____
_____
_____
_____
_____

Answers to Pacing Yourself: a. Poor; b. Good; c. Good; d. Poor; e. Good.

Unit 4 Performance Mastery

Name _____ Date _____

Working Vocabulary

Briefly define or identify each of the following terms. In the space provided, write your definitions or identifications using your own words. [Numbers refer to chapters where terms are introduced or discussed.]

Bias [16, 17] _____

_____

Defensive [17] _____

_____

Disabled [15] _____

_____

Discrimination [15, 17] _____

_____

EEOC [15, 17] _____

_____

Ethnic group [15, 17] _____

_____

Majority [15, 17] _____

_____

Minority [15, 17] _____

_____

Patronize [17] _____

_____

Pluralistic society [15] _____

_____

Prejudice [16, 17] _____

_____

Protected classes [15] _____

_____

Stereotype [16, 17] _____

_____

Discussion

In the space provided, write your answers to these questions using your own words.

a. How are the ways African-Americans and Native Americans came to be in the United States different from the way others did?_____

_____

_____

b. Give examples of how we belong to more than one group at the same time?

_____

_____

c. What are some advantages to belonging to a group? What are some dangers?

_____

_____

_____

d. List as many different groups that make up this country as you can. _____

_____

_____

_____

e. Under the law, which groups are classified as minorities and which as protected classes? _____

_____

_____

f. Why is it to bad to use stereotypes? _____

_____

_____

_____

g. What are three guidelines for avoiding the use of stereotypes?_____

_____

_____

h. What are some mistakes people make in trying to avoid prejudice? _____

_____

_____

i. What are some things a minority-group member can do to maintain good human relations when being discriminated against? _____

_____

_____

_____

Name _____   Date _____

Performance Assessment One

Your goal in this assessment is to develop an awareness of your own biases as well as your use of stereotypes.

With the help of friends and relatives, answer questions about your background and views as honestly and thoroughly as you can. Use the information to write a report, on a separate sheet of paper, about your strengths and weaknesses in dealing with groups different from yours. In your report, include the following facts:

1. Identify the various groups to which you belong: (a) Racial (b) Ethnic (c) Geographic—Northerner, Southerner, Westerner, and so on (d) Religious (e) Economic (f) Age (g) Sex (h) Other.

2. Identify the general biases and stereotypes held by the groups to which you belong. Identify stereotypes others hold about members of your group. Try to explain how they developed or what reasons are given for them.

3. Identify special biases and stereotypes that you have developed as a result of your background and experiences. Try to show how you got these ideas.

4. State how much experience you have had in working or interacting with members of groups different from yours.

5. Describe any situations in which you have been involved in which biases and stereotyped thinking hurt human relations. (You may have been the victim or the one showing the bias, or both at once.)

6. Describe any situations you know of in which you or others tried to overcome the effects of bias and stereotypes.

Performance Assessment Two

Your goal in this assessment is to learn how various groups have worked to wipe out biases and stereotyped thinking to improve human relations in your community, the country, or the world.

Interview representatives of various organizations and agencies. A few suggested organizations and agencies are listed below, and there are many others. Look for answers to the questions listed below and others that you can think of that affect your own community. On a separate sheet of paper, write a brief report showing what has been attempted, what has been accomplished, and what still remains to be done.

Organizations, agencies, and other sources to check are:

Church groups
Interracial groups
Human relations councils
National Association for the Advancement of Colored People (NAACP)
National Organization for Women (NOW)
National Conference of Christians and Jews
Anti-Defamation League of B'nai B'rith
Neighborhood Settlement houses
Social service agencies
Equal Employment Opportunity Commission (EEOC) or state or city agency
Human Rights Commission of your state or city
American Civil Liberties Union
Groups for disabled people

Questions to ask are

a. Why was the group formed?
b. What are the most important things in people's attitudes that must be changed to overcome biases?
c. What specific activities has the group sponsored to bring about greater understanding among different groups?
d. What are some of the groups the organization works with?
e. What success has the group had?
f. What special problems does the group face?
g. How would the group assess its situation today, as opposed to what it was like 10, 25, and 50 years ago?